Musings

Musings

Reflections on Being

Edward L. Boye

Foreword by
Fred B. Craddock

RESOURCE *Publications* · Eugene, Oregon

MUSINGS
Reflections on Being

Copyright © 2014 Edward L. Boye. All rights reserved. Except for brief quotations in critical publications or reviews, no part of this book may be reproduced in any manner without prior written permission from the publisher. Write: Permissions. Wipf and Stock Publishers, 199 W. 8th Ave., Suite 3, Eugene, OR 97401.

Resource Publications
An Imprint of Wipf and Stock Publishers
199 W. 8th Ave., Suite 3
Eugene, OR 97401

www.wipfandstock.com

ISBN 13: 978-1-62564-682-8

Manufactured in the U.S.A. 09/08/2014

Dedication

I want to dedicate this book in memory of my father, the Reverend Lee Olin Boye, who taught me critical thinking. He challenged me to not just accept what I read or what I heard, but to think the subject matter through, seek the sources, question the authenticity, and then make it my own.

Table of Contents

Foreward by Fred B. Craddock — xi
Preface — xv
Acknowledgments — xvii

The Muse	1
Growing Old	2
God and Beyond	3
Afterlife?	4
God is Love	5
Science versus Spirituality	6
Perfection	6
The "No-No" World	7
Listening	8
Stuff	8
This Babe in the Straw	9
Transition	10
The Good Old Days	11
Do Trees Cry?	12
The Morning After	12
Angels and Demons	13
Moments	14
It's a Mad, Mad, Mad, Mad World	15
Contagious Compassion	16
Pack Time	16
Time to Punt	17
The Boot	18
And This Too Shall Pass	19
Mine, All Mine	19
Heaven On Earth	20
The Ultimate Ride	21
No Mistakes	22
Tough Atonement	23
Trading Places	24
Choices	24
Alive or Dead	25
"Skin on"	26
We Know	27
You Are Me. I Am You.	28
Things	29
Too Little Time	30
Sands of Time	31
Where is Happiness?	32
The Listening Heart	33
To See or Not to See	34
Identity Crisis	35
Feet of Clay	36
Beside Oneself	37
Living Mirror	38
Unlikely Angels	39
Old Souls	40
Images	41
Chaos	42
Sacred Dirt	43

Table of Contents

Life is Difficult	44
Oh, to be Heard	45
Humor	46
The Bigger Picture	47
Savoring Life	48
Measuring Up	49
Repetition	49
That Which We Cannot Know	50
The Beauty of the Journey	51
Perspective	52
Word Power	53
But I Have To!	53
Totally Free!	54
Personal Review	55
Simpler Choices	56
Taking the Blinders Off	57
Street People	58
The Loudness of Silence	59
Temptation	60
Do You Know Me?	61
Nothing But Net	62
Epidemic Rage	63
Self-Importance	64
Enchantment	65
Sacred Ground: Part I	66
Sacred Ground: Part II	67
False Gods	68
Sitting in the Ashes	69
The Home	70
Where is the Field Manual?	71
Honoring Your Body	72
Freedom From Fear	73
Retirement?	74
When Love Rules	75
Resourcefulness	76
A Living Novel	77
Certainty or Risk?	78
Voices	79
God's Will	80
More Than I Anticipated	81
Saved from the Monster	82
Rabbits and Eggs??	83
What Matters in the End?	84
Religious Superiority	85
The Power of Touch	86
Powerful Words	87
Living Responsibly	88
Refreshing Honesty	88
Embodiment of Hate	89
The Unbearable Lightness of Being	90
Then Face To Face	91
The Law of Three	92
Going with the Flow	92
Beyond the Obvious	93
Balance	94
Truly Rich	95
An Enchanting Story	96
Respecting Our Elders	97
Que, Sera, Sera	98
Joy	98
Celebrity Status	99
The *Internet* is a Lonely Hunter	100
A Singing Heart	101
Encompassing Differences	102
Life Can Be Messy	103
Doubt	104
Kissing Frogs!	105
The New Deity?	106
No Time To Reflect	107
God's Promise	108
Touch	108
The Great Leap	109
Falling Short	110

Table of Contents

Deal of A Lifetime!	111
Roots	112
Timeout	113
Circadian Muddle	113
Missed Gifts	114
The Good Ending	115
Releasing Spirits	115
Heartfelt	116
A Time To Release	117
The Benefits of Taking Time	118
Choice	119
Crisis and Thrill Junkies	119
Truth	120
Detours	121
"If Only"	122
The Jesus I Never Knew	123
Larger Than Life	124
"May the Force be with You"	125
Prayer	126
Against the Tide	127
"Barn Raisin'"	127
Tiredness to Tenacity	128
Balance	129
Stories	130
Smiles or Tears	131
Castles in the Air	132
Caring versus Caring For	133
When I Am Old and Feeble	134
"Ya Hear Now?"	135
Exposed	135
Beauty or Beast	136
Perturbation	137
Beyond Greeting: Part I	138
Beyond Greeting: Part II	139
Bought and Paid For	140
Fame and Fortune	140
Plan B	141
A Profound Wisdom	142
Stories	143
"Set-R-Down"	144
Strangely Warmed	144
Teachers and Educators	145
Good Purpose	146
Possibility	147
Time	147
Waiting for the Worm	149
Potty Mouth	150
Badges of Life	151
Wednesday Again	151
Look Before You Leap	152
Treasures in Plain Sight	153
Best of Everything	154
Iron-Clad Contract	155
Overwhelmed!	156
Our Best Teacher	156
Resentment	157
Silent Shame	158
Great Expectations	159
Can You Hear the Quiet?	160
Little Teacher, Big Lessons	161
The Wounded Caretaker	162
Help in Time of Need	163
Peace and Quiet: Part I	164
Peace and Quiet: Part II	165
The Wizard of Widgets	166
Thorns and Clay	166
Oh, the Innocence of Childhood	167
I Wish	168
Whitewashing Fences	169
The Drive to Control	170
The Charmed Ones	171
Open Mouth . . .	172
Not What It Seems	172
Living with the Enemy	173
Simple Love	174

Table of Contents

Our Unwieldy Body	175
Labor Day	175
The Whole Picture	175
Smiles	176
I Can't Wait!	177
Health Through Movement	178
Living with Grace	179
Thieves of Opportunity	179
"Everything is Beautiful"	180
Time in the Desert	181
"It's the God's Truth"	182
Be Here Now	182
Epilogue–Catfish, Cornbread, and "Crazy" People	187
Bibliography	191

Foreword

I am confident that Ed's choice of *Musings* as the title for these reflections was not a claim to inspired speech. I think he means that these are reflections on life as he has and is experiencing it, no more, no less. He stakes no claim that the Muse, the spirit or power which is said to visit poets and artists, visited him. The overall modesty of these pages says No to such a claim. But neither can he deny it. Wisdom does not usually call attention to itself. "Out of the mouths of babies and infants." (Psalm 8:2) I will not embarrass Ed by discussing this further, but both the writer and the reader must be open in mind and in heart for the truth to be spoken and heard. Truth enters the marketplace of ideas in humility, let others tag it as they will.

The ancient Greeks who seemed to have the capacity to sit on their own shoulders and reflect on life while living it, called such activity "Musing." "Musing" they said, "was the daughter of memory." They did not equate Musing and Memory, for while Memory is required for Musing, Memory is a larger and more inclusive term. At its base is the exercise of depositing and retrieving information. "Nashville is the capital of Tennessee" is a bit of information which I may store in the caverns of my mind just in case I may at some time need to bring it to surface. A teacher may ask for it or it may appear as a question on an exam. This exercise is called Recall, the capacity to retrieve from the past and bring into the present.

Memory also includes an exercise less demanding. This we call Recognition. If Recall is bringing something from the past into the present (Deposit/Retrieval), Recognition is taking something in the present and locating it in its proper part. I may not be able to *recall* that the capital of Tennessee is Nashville, but if you gave me a list of six cities, I can *recognize* which one is the capital of Tennessee. Recognition is easier than recall; it is no wonder students prefer multiple-choice tests. In this exercise of memory

Foreword

there is a great deal of pleasure; it is learning what we already know. It generates and sustains conversation because we can recognize enough of the subject matter to participate and to contribute to it.

But there is a third order of memory which is even less demanding than recognition; this we call *reverie*. In reverie we are free from restraints of time, place, cause and effect, and cast of characters. The mind floats as one reads or listens, in the course of which we may be taken to places we have never been and have a feeling of familiarity; we may return to places we have known and have a feeling of strangeness. By no means is such remembering a waste of time; out of it comes inventions, poetry, visions of new worlds, new alliances, changes of character and lifestyle. And more.

On the spectrum from recall to reverie lies *Musing*, located closer to reverie than to recall. Recall and recognition provide raw material for reflection, pondering, meditating, loitering, browsing, ruminating, musing. Ed moves comfortably across this spectrum with intimate distance. A strength of his writing is that he muses about times, places, events, and relationships common to us all. As we begin to read the topics are Ed's, but before long they are ours. Or so it seems. I think Ed would have it no other way. He is not trying to sell us something nor does he have to dwell on the remarkable or hyperbolic in order to hold our attention. Musing on the way life is is pleasurable. Even boredom can be interesting. Of course, not all topics are equidistant from our thoughts and feelings. You will discover some musings are as familiar as your own front yard which others are as strange as the dark side of the moon. But maybe not: linger longer. My guess is that on most pages you could write in the margin, 'I think Ed has been reading my mail." In any case, there are in these musings no reason to be suspicious; were there any hidden agenda, trust would be broken and communication would stop. But I trust Ed's work, clear or vague, just as I would trust him to feed my cat when I am away or to pick up the kids after soccer practice.

For reading these musings, I offer three suggestions. One, do not try to impose a structure or an outline on these reflections; they are by nature at random. They do not yield to frames any more than poetry does, or sermons do. Two, read these musings one at a time. Their value is not in accumulation. If one does not stir you, it cannot be redeemed by the next one. And finally, slow down and relax. Musings are for walking not running, for hammocks not motorcycles. Sören Kierkegaard tells of a man so anxious and tense that his physician ordered one full day of rest. Relax;

unwind. The patient thanked his physician and a few weeks later reported that he felt better. "But," he said, "I found I could relax so fast that I was through by noon."

Thanks, Ed

Dr. Fred B. Craddock

Bandy Professor of Preaching and New Testament, Emeritus
Emory University, Atlanta, Georgia

Cherry Log, Georgia
June 2014

Preface

I am a thinker, explorer, listener, and storyteller. Life is truly fascinating to me. It is dynamic, always changing, and full of surprises. This book, "Musings" is about the wonders of life, living, and being. These writings evolved from years of reading "human novels", the study of many topics and personal reflections. I am a sponge for information.

In the fall of 2011, a friend started emailing me daily articles written by an ordained Disciples of Christ minister in South Georgia. I immediately felt a connection to the author. I could tell we had a kinship in our earthly journeys. I replied to one of his articles and shared with him that I had been writing my thoughts about life for some years. He encouraged me to share those thoughts and experiences with my friends and became one of my subscribers. So, in December 2011 *Musings: Reflections on Being* was born.

I wish I could say I enjoyed writing term papers, articles, sermons, or my dissertation. This was different. The words just seemed to come from nowhere. Most mornings when I sat before the computer still half asleep, I would suddenly become wide awake. Thoughts started pouring onto the screen. I knew then the existence of an artistic Muse.

It has truly been a joy to write about philosophy, psychology, living, thinking, being, and at times something whimsical or the occasional poem. Many of my email subscribers passed them on to their friends. Their feedback, constructive critique and praise have inspired me to continue.

So much of traditional literature has a beginning and an ending. These musings have a beginning, but their endings are left to you, if you choose to continue. I suggest reading each musing one at a time. Spend some time thinking it through, before going on to the next. Some musings will not speak to you, so move on. A few will sound like repeats. If you are like me, I often see the same thing in a different light on a new day. You may want

Preface

to let a musing live in you for a day or two to see if it will become bread for your journey. If just one musing inspires you to make a change that leads to positive results, that feeling or action will affect others and has the potential of reverberating around the world.

Musings is about "being" . . . taking time to experience the moment. Learning to just "be" can be a challenge in our fast-paced, often competitive society. May these musings and the reflections they inspire lead to blessings in your life and to those whose lives you touch.

In addition to the musings, I've included a short story as an epilogue to this book entitled "Catfish, Cornbread, and Crazy People." It is a true story about the essence of community. It is one of the spiritual highlights of my life.

Dr. Edward L. Boye
June 2014

Acknowledgments

This is the part of a book that most people breeze through or skip altogether. However, it is a significant part of any book. It acknowledges the foundation of the book . . . addressing many of the people who inspired or contributed in some way to the writing. No book is written by one person. It is a team effort. I want to introduce you to my team.

My love of knowledge and reading grew from seeds planted by my mother, the late Betty Margaret Armbrister Boye. She was a voracious reader and read stories to me and my two sisters.

The flames for this love of knowledge and reading were fanned by my father, the late Reverend Lee Olin Boye, who introduced me at a young age to critical thinking. He wouldn't let me off the hook with quick answers. We would sit for hours at the kitchen table while he challenged me with questions about philosophy, theology, and life in general. He always encouraged me to ask why. By asking why, I developed my own beliefs and thoughts and the ability not to accept blindly what others handed down. I am sure I caused my teachers some grey hair.

I want to thank Dr. Fred Craddock for challenging me one Sunday by saying, "Ed, if you write a page a day for three hundred and sixty five days, you will have a book." (Fred, you didn't tell me that after the three hundred and sixty five days, that's when the work really begins!)

The late Dale Andrews, author of *Things I Say To Myself,* encouraged me to open the files of thoughts and ideas I had accumulated and share them with others. Thus was the birth of *Musings: Reflections on Being.*

Dr. Beth Roberts, Professor Emerita of Education at Oglethorpe University in Atlanta, Georgia and one of my readers, told me one day she was keeping all of the email *Musings* in a file on her computer. She asked

Acknowledgments

whether I would like for her to edit them. I am indebted to her for the first editing of work. This was the beginning of my publishing thoughts.

I attended the fiftieth reunion of my high school graduating class in 2013. In a conversation with one of my classmates, she learned about the *Musings* and requested to be on the email list. When I got home and sent her the first musing, she sent it back corrected with an apology that she couldn't restrain herself. She has a degree in Theology and in Law which proved helpful throughout. Marion Van Gelder Henson, M.Div., JD, this book would not be going to the publisher without your tenacity in correcting the grammar and punctuation. You have been an inspiration and a great teacher in how to write with clarity.

Great appreciation and humble gratitude goes to Matthew Wimer, the Managing Editor at Wipf and Stock Publishers for guiding me through the process.

I would also like to thank my two sisters, Patty Gillenwater, and Linda Shafer. Were it not for them, I wouldn't have developed my imagination, weird sense of humor, and survival skills. They are always there for me with their love and support and make sure I keep my stories straight.

Behind every person taking on the monumental task of writing a book is that one person who inspires courage and dedication. That person is my lovely wife, Julia Ann Purcell. She was instrumental in getting me through my last graduate degree by editing my dissertation and relentlessly pushing me through the seemingly unending process of rewrites. With this book she has been patient whenever I have been lost in the world of writing. She has been the voice of reason and has given me her quiet support through the process of coming up with the manuscript. She was there as I came down the stretch to edit several last minute additions and put in a very long week editing and fine-tuning the manuscript.

Finally, I would like to thank all the readers of the email distributions of *Musings* who shared how they had been inspired, offered ideas for change, and expressed words of gratitude and support.

Edward L. Boye, D.Min.
June 2014

Musings

The Muse

What is the Muse? We find in literature that there many muses. "The muses ... in Greek mythology, poetry, and literature, are the goddesses of inspiration in literature, science, and the arts." [1]

More specifically, the muse or muses are spirit guides or spiritual inspiration. The content of my writing arises from such spirit guides and spiritual inspiration. I am always amazed when I sit down at my computer and write. It is as if someone is guiding my hand as I type.

I believe we all have the ability to tap into such resources, whether we desire to write, paint, sculpt, build buildings, garden, or create in any other way. Whatever we undertake will be a beautiful creation if we are willing to believe in the guidance of something greater than ourselves, and something beyond this earthly realm.

Our ability to create is a gift that we may take for granted. Even what seems to be a simple task of preparing a meal is an expression of creativity. (Sometimes we rush through it or think "Oh no, I have to cook again.") We start with ingredients from many different people, from the person who planted the seed and harvested the fruit, from the one who cooked, canned, and packaged it, who shipped it to a store, who priced it and put on the shelf . . . all for us to buy. We spend time turning these ingredients into creations with flavor to be taken into our bodies not only to nourish us, but also to delight and give us pleasure.

We used to say no one could cook like Mama. That's because there was a lot of love put into preparing each meal. Mama felt led to make those dishes the best that she could out of love for her family. We learned to love what she made for us. (Well, almost. I never did like brussel sprouts no matter what Mama did to them!)

In order to experience each creation by our hands and/or brains, we have to be focused on what we are doing. We have to be aware that something spiritual within ourselves blossoms into creative ideas. We have to be "mindful," i.e., "the quality or state of being conscious or aware of something . . .focusing one's awareness on the present moment . . ." [2] To be mindful is to see what we are creating as being the best we can make it and to see it as a gift to the world. If we infuse our creations with love and are

---

1. Wikipedia, "Muse."
2. Oxford Dictionary, "Mindful."

open to the inspiration of forces greater than ourselves, the beauty of those creations will illuminate those who are blessed by their presence.

It doesn't matter how small a task we are involved in. If the work we do is seen as a gift to those around us, then our work is a creation of beauty and value. Unfortunately, our world seems more focused on the sensational than the ordinary. That might even cause us to think that the ordinary isn't important and without value. This couldn't be further from the truth. Pay attention and you will see what we do is never ordinary. What we do with love and with a giving heart is a miracle of creation.

Invite the muse to walk with you in all that you create! You will be amazed at how different the world will look.

Growing Old

I often hear about the internal struggles of persons in retirement who want to continue contributing to life. I include myself in this group. I do look at my life and know that I have already contributed a lot as shown by my "already experienced bucket list". (I have listed experiences of what I have learned, done, and am to affirm that I have lived life large.) Yet, I and others with whom I have talked still have the need to generate and contribute to life, to the world, and to others.

Is there a point in life where one should be content to sit back and reminisce, reliving accomplishments and experiences in one's mind, sharing with others of bygone days, just waiting for death? Maybe there is a phase of living in which we learn just to be in the moment, whatever the age. Maybe this is the slow transition from being an earthly being to a spiritual being. As I grow older, my thinking has moved to more philosophical and theological questions than ever before. I have many questions. Is there life beyond death? Is there reunion with family and friends who have gone before us? Or do we beings of energy just join the sea of energy floating in the universe? Am I missing the presence of God by focusing on how I think God should make Him/Herself known at any particular moment?

And can anyone ever really write about or make sense of the process of aging? Because those who do write about aging are often in the process of aging and perhaps have less opportunity for an objective perspective! One would have to stand outside life itself to gain that perspective. And maybe the man of Nazareth spoke to just this: life and death and the possibility of life again. Ask Him as you are walking your road to Damascus!

God and Beyond

One traditional belief about a God somewhere beyond our physical senses revolves around the concepts of the Trinity, the virgin birth, and the life and resurrection of Jesus. Given the prevalence of that view and my studies, there is a part of me that thinks those events could be possible. An omniscient supreme being/higher power could possibly have created a situation 2000 years ago to cause us to take note about how we can live better, and how we can connect at a spiritual and loving level. The story of Jesus is so outrageous from what we experience in the structure of life as we know it, that it causes us to take notice.

On the other hand, I seem to be leaning in the direction that the traditional model doesn't make sense. The creation story in Genesis has often been labeled a myth without foundation by scientists. This Biblical story and many others were written in a time when humanity had only its imagination to create answers to explain or help understand life. I have thought for a long time that it doesn't make sense that a baby could be conceived without a sperm and an egg. Why would a creator leave out one half of his or her ability to create? Also, if God came into the world in the form of a man, why would he not experience the love of another person of creation which would include not only Agape love, which was apparent, but also Eros, a significant and completing form of love?

Do we have any examples of such happenings today that are beyond our ability to explain that they would make international news and cause intense scientific study? This makes me believe that people 2000 years ago used what limited knowledge they had in an attempt to explain what they didn't understand.

At the age of seventy, I also have a lot of questions about death motivated by the limited years of this existence that are left to me. Will there be awareness as we know it beyond death? If so, we would have to take with us the feelings we have now which include pain, sadness, grief, and anger, as well as joy, happiness, and contentment. How can we know one without the other to contrast? There are aspects of my personality that I want to be rid of, e.g., greed, hate, entitlement, egotism, etc. And yet there are desires to be able to reconnect with persons I have loved deeply who have transcended this existence to whatever spiritual form there may be.

I follow Blaise Pascal's struggle with understanding life.

> "God is, or He is not." But to which side shall we incline? Reason can decide nothing here. There is an infinite chaos which separated us. A game is being played at the extremity of his infinite distance where heads or tails will turn up ... Which will you choose then? Let us see. Since you must choose, let us see which interests you least. You have two things to lose, the true and the good; and two things to stake, your reason and your will, your knowledge and your happiness; and your nature has two things to shun, error and misery. Your reason is no more shocked in choosing one rather than the other, since you must of necessity choose ... But your happiness? Let us weigh the gain and the loss in wagering that God is.... If you gain, you gain all; if you lose, you lose nothing. Wager, then, without hesitation that He is."[3]

Blaise Pascal essentially said that we have two choices: to believe in God and an afterlife or to believe that when we die, we cease to exist. As we see, he decided that the best gamble was to believe in an afterlife. As a friend of mine said that it is the best lottery ticket he has!

So I, like Pascal, echo the statement of the man in the Bible: "I do believe; help me overcome my unbelief." (Mark 9:24)

It is good to walk this path with fellow sojourners. May your day be filled with signs of deity!

Afterlife?

When are we most content? What fills us with joy? For most of us, it's when we are truly connected with another human being by love, a place that words truly fail to describe. Love is a bonding experience that feels like we have stepped outside of the normal everyday world. It is when we have a connection of souls, a total focus on the moment. Everything else seems not to exist. Even writing about this, I feel a bubbling up of a sense of warmth, happiness, and security.

When are we at the worst depths of pain and hopeless? Many would say it's when we feel totally apart from others, isolated in a way that only total darkness can come close to describing. Other such experiences include betrayal, rejection, self-loathing, hate, etc. These are states of being when we feel totally cut off from any feelings of connection with others. Maybe

---

3. Pascal, *Penses* #233.

suicide is the ultimate act of cutting oneself away from all souls. Putting the pen to this feels cold and terrifying.

Most (I am an optimist) people spend a lifetime working toward shedding feelings and behaviors that cut them off from others. We look for ways to feel better about life and ourselves, and ways to love others.

Maybe the afterlife is joining a body of energy, of spiritual connectedness, where we have leave behind all of the negative feelings and behaviors that bring on those experiences of isolation. A man by the name of Paul said something to the effect that we are the body of the church, one part being no more important than another, with something unique about the head, and yet all still a part of the body! (1 Corinthians 12:12–31)

God Is Love

I am not sure tackling this topic can be defined clearly. "God" and "love" are two words that defy simple explanations or definitions. However, no one ever said I was one to shy away from a challenge. At best, I can offer you my understanding of the title of this musing.

Love is the word most used to describe God. In academic and especially theological circles, there are other frequently-used phrases, such as God is omnipresent (always with us, or one could say "in the moment"), God is omniscient, (all-knowing), and God is omnipotent (all powerful). All of these words suggest that God isn't a contained being. The scripture states, "God created mankind in his own image." However, many of us create an image of God in a male body with our same skin color. God becomes an individual, a physical body, and contained in one place.

I stated in a previous musing that most of us feel peak joy and contentment when we are deeply connected by love with another human being. And when a group bonds, each member is in sync with the others, and joy abounds. The group and God become one and is no longer a group of individuals. The group becomes one through love. "For where two or three are gathered in my name, there I am with them." (Matt 18:20) "And the two shall become one flesh." (Mark 10:7a)

There will be sightings of God today. I hope you are there to experience them.

Musings

Science versus Spirituality

The big debate these days involves science and spirituality. I don't use "religion" in these musings because religion is a set of beliefs that are confined within specific doctrine. In contrast, spirituality is without physicality, the opposite of the traditional definition of science.

There is definitely an experience of otherworldliness in this journey called "life." Fredrick Buechner addresses these realms as he comments on dreams:

> "...we are in constant touch with a world that is as real to us while we are in it and has as much to do with who we are, and whose ultimate origin and destiny are as unknown and fascinating, as the world of waking reality.... Maybe the Real World is not the only reality, and even if it should turn out to be, maybe they [those who are stuck in their surety of science] are not really looking at it realistically."[4]

Of course, dreams are not the only experience where we step into a different realm. There is something surreal in the sudden awe-inspiring experience of seeing a thing of beauty, for example, a bird with bright plumage, a bright red or yellow tree in autumn standing by itself, the birthing of a baby, etc.

Most scientists are short-sighted. They see only what the eye can see. They measure only what they can touch. They are confined to their prison of the empirical. When they are presented with something that defies the empirical, they often say "we just have not been able to discover the answer yet".

To be spiritual is to look beyond what is obvious, what is material, what is measurable. The beyond is made up of such things as love, faith, belief, trust, honor, and imagination.

May you be able to take a peek today into a world beyond the horizon!

Perfection

The word "perfection" can be a weight around our necks. As we aspire to it, it becomes a "carrot on a stick." We never quite reach it. The most common definition of perfection is "without flaw." No matter what we do, how hard and long we work, we seem not to reach that place where we feel "perfect." There seems to be one more thing we can do to reach that place

---

4. Buechner, *Whistling*, 38.

where we feel satisfied with where we are and who we are. But we never get there because there is always "one more thing"! Oh, we are doomed to be flawed. Yet wasn't it Jesus who said, "Why do you call me good? No one is good—except God alone." (Mark 10:18) We could infer that Jesus was saying that even he himself was not without flaw! However, we continue to beat ourselves up for not reaching that "carrot" that dangles out of reach. This mindset is an injustice to our peace and happiness!

Let me share with you a different definition of perfection: "Being able to accept where you are in the moment as a state of perfection." All we really have is "Now." Yesterday is but a thought filed in the banks of our neurons. Tomorrow's dreams and hope are also floating about in our "grey matter." Therefore, all we really have is right where we are in this second. Being able to accept "what is" at the moment is as perfect as it can be. Knowing this can free us to enjoy the moment, to be, to savor aliveness, no matter what the circumstance. There are truly times when we don't want to be where we are, such as when we are experiencing grief, pain, fear, etc. And, yet here we are. What can being here teach us? "Here" is a perfect place to learn about life.

I think I will go out and smell the roses, thorns and all.

The "No-No" World

We are curious creatures. We are fascinated by this world and all the variety in it. We can never experience or know about all that it holds. We are pleasantly surprised when we see a new insect, plant, or animal discovered by science. We are awed by every new sunset even though we have seen hundreds or thousands of them.

We come out of the womb with curiosity. It is how we learn to navigate life, and yet, there are big tall creatures running around behind us yelling, "No-no," "Don't touch," "Don't put that in your mouth," "Don't put the cat in the refrigerator," etc. And then there are the "shoulds". "You should wear clean underwear; you don't know when you will be in an accident." I always thought if I were in an accident my clean underwear was a goner anyway! Yes, we need guidance and the wisdom of experience, but we need it to be given in love and not in fear.

If we have been guided only with admonitions and not with love, we grow up with a fear of trying new things. We have a tape loop in our brain saying, "You should do this," and "You should do that." This puts us in a state of "shoulding" all over ourselves. We become limited and overly cautious, and we often have negative feelings about what is natural.

The Bible invites us to be child-like. (Matt 8:13) Jesus was fascinated by and honored children. (Matt 19:14) He cautioned against harming them.

Maybe we come with some wisdom already within. It just needs to be cultivated in the presence of love. The joy of life is finding something to be awed by every day!

What wonders will today hold for us?

Listening

We live in a world of constant buzz. We have become stimulus junkies, so hearing is separated from absorbing. With email, iPhones, iPads, eReaders, and other types of writing and reading devices, we don't have much opportunity to engage in just listening. Unfortunately, some of our role models are radio "shock jocks" and politicians, both of whom feign listening but seem to be caught up in their own self-serving agendas.

I often find myself in a group where some of us (and that includes me) seem to be in a verbal wrestling match to see who can dominate and win the coveted "belt" for smartest, most clever, and most enlightened. How can we really listen when the noise in our heads is planning the next thing to say?

As a child spending time on my grandmother's farm, I had to feed the chickens. I always thought it was funny to watch them all "clucking" at the same time. I wondered what they were saying and to whom. I guess they could have been expressing gratitude to me for the feed. I don't know. I don't speak chicken, except when I am in a group of people, and I can assure you the conversation is rarely about expressing gratitude.

I like the expression; "God gave us two ears and one mouth. He must have been telling us something!" And Jesus tells us several times to focus on our hearing, "He who has ears let him hear." (Matt 11:15)

I have a lot of respect for the quiet people. Often, when they do speak, they say something profound.

Stuff

Christmas season may not be the best time of the year to talk about this topic. And yet, it may be the best time for the conversation. We have become a consumer nation. When I hear the phrase, "consumer nation," it reminds me of a movie scene in which farmers in the West watched an invasion of locusts devour every green thing in sight.

We are shocked at the sights we see on the television program, *Hoarders*. Tickets for some of the talk shows at Christmas are almost impossible to get because the hosts are giving away a truck load of stuff to the audiences.

There is a trend of late to live with less, although the trend is small compared to the enthusiasm for the desire to have more. We read articles about "downsizing" and living a simpler life style. There is even a magazine called *Real Simple*.

I visited a home recently. When I walked in, there was a sense of lightness and freedom. When I commented on the beauty of their home, the homeowners explained that they were minimalists. It wasn't a Spartan existence but it was truly beautiful and refreshing, especially for someone with attention deficit disorder often agitated by clutter.

I still struggle in determining the difference between "need" and "want." There is still a little boy in me who has a strong desire for new "toys."

This giving of things was all started by three wise guys long ago. And yet, the focus then was to honor a Savior who had come to save us from ourselves. When we look upon this scene in a cattle stall, our eyes are only open to see what the wisemen are bringing. Could we be missing something? I share a poem with you.

This Babe in the Straw

>A star in the sky leads to a miraculous event
>Wise men and shepherds didn't know what it meant
>As they came close they were in awe
>They found a lowly Babe lying in the straw
>
>Oh wondrous child who before wise men kneel
>And radiant peace did those shepherds feel
>Mom and dad in state of awe
>With their Babe lying upon the straw

Musings

Oh, the fate of the ages he did not know
Yet, a force to reckon with he did grow
To his warmth people would draw
To this beautiful Babe lying in the straw

He grew to be wise beyond his years
The priests of the temple were in shock as he opened their ears
He challenged their book upon which was written the law
This lowly Babe lying in the straw

If we choose to draw near
He will take from us all our fear
Our pain will be cast out that is so raw
In the presence of this Babe in the straw

Their fear drove them to hang him on a cross
They accused him of crimes that were false
Even death did not defeat him as they saw
This miraculous Babe lying in the straw.

—Edward L. Boye, 2013

Transition

We usually think of transition in situations of job changes, major illness, moving, marriage, etc. These are important transitions. They change our lives. Each of us needs time and understanding to process major life changes in our own unique way. Everyone processes change differently, so it takes compassion and patience from ourselves and from those around us to be able to absorb what is new.

We are often unaware of how we may be impacted by smaller transitions. We may think there will be no impact when we come home and the furniture has moved to a different configuration. In the middle of the night our legs and shins will show us differently! We become accustomed to doing the same tasks the same way automatically without thinking. Even a small transition may stop us in our tracks when someone changes how something is done or moves cabinet contents to a different place in the kitchen.

One of the most difficult transitions is during the early years of a divorce as children go from one home to another. Life always works differently in each home. When the children first arrive at either home, there is often some acting out. They aren't being bad or difficult. They just need time to change "gears" in their thinking. They need some quality and loving time and sometimes, reminders of the process in that home.

Another significant transition is going to and arriving from an extended stay like a vacation. My wife and I often sit in the car for a few minutes when leaving and when we arrive back home to give our bodies and minds time to "be here now."

Take time to observe the transitions in life. Will life have less stress? Who knows? You might see something different!

The Good Old Days

Every now and then, we hear people say, "I wish we could go back to the good old days." I think the desire for the "good old days" is a desire for life to be simpler and slower. We focus on images of Currier and Ives, Norman Rockwell, and Thomas Kincade. Their paintings look inviting, loving, warm, and cozy.

Winter provides an opportunity to create moments of simply being. We can sit, watch the snow fall and the sun reflecting on the glistening crystals. I am always amazed as I stand out in the snow that time and sound seem to change. It's like nature is providing sound-proofing for our busy world. There is a quiet, slow, peace about the snow.

I am writing this on December 21st, the winter solstice, the shortest day and the longest night of the year. It is a time of winding down from the year, having a night of "human hibernation" with the chance of rejuvenation for the coming season.

This is a prime opportunity for restorative activities like taking naps, reading a good book, savoring good food, stretching (imitate your cat or dog), soaking in a hot bubble bath, or simply being aware of our breathing. Fix a cup of mulled cider, hot toddy, or hot chocolate to sit and sip as the cup warms your hands. Build a fire in the fireplace or wood stove for an opportunity to be mesmerized by the dancing flames. These days you can even have a simulated fireplace on your TV!

As the rest of the earth seems to retreat and prepare for the next cycle of life, so can we.

Musings

Do Trees Cry?

Is there a clear separation between what is spirit and what is material? Are inanimate objects without life? The Native Americans, among others, believe that all things possess spirit. Yes, they even include rocks, water, wood, and air. We can feel movement of the air and see the result of its "aliveness". We can see and feel the "aliveness" of water. Master carpenters would say that a beautiful piece of cherry or walnut has life. They talk about bringing out the living grain.

I am no master craftsman, but when I work with wood, I have experienced life evolving before my eyes as I coax a beautiful piece of wood into a finished table or a fine jewelry box. This box then holds "jewels" whose beauty dazzles as the sun bathes their facets into aliveness. A stone sculptor sees life in the stone as well. When asked what he was doing with a large block of stone, Michelangelo said, ". . .there is an angel inside of this rock and I am setting him free."[5]

We have been told that we have been given dominion over all the earth. Dominion essentially means the power to govern, which means the power to influence or guide. There is no mention of possessing, seizing, or taking . . . all of which end in destruction.

If we could see each *thing* around us with spirit, we might take more care, have more compassion. If we are truly created in the image of God, then we are co-creators. And as we create, love often is transferred to the creation. Love and destruction cannot exist in the same space!

Do trees cry? You tell me.

The Morning After

The little boy inside me still likes to get presents. However, the more practical side of me knows that I know better what I want than anyone else does. So, some years ago, my wife and I decided to change our traditional approach to giving presents for Christmas. We buy our "Christmas" at the time we need (or sometimes) want during the year. And I have to admit, it gives me a feeling of freedom during the holiday season not to be caught up in manic consumer mentality. I think it must also give our loved ones some comfort not to be pressed to come up with something they think we would like.

5. Widener, *Angel,* 10.

I'm not a Scrooge. You ask, "What about your grandchildren?" Though they may not know it now, I know when they begin paying for college they will thoroughly enjoy the increasing interest from gifts placed in the bank.

Consider the similarity of the words *presents* and *presence*. For me, "presence" is the essence of the celebration that sometimes gets lost in the mounds of "presents", wrapping paper, and decorations. That presence of years ago has made a difference in the way I act and see the world. For me, it is the motivation for giving to needs outside myself all year long.

Without having to worry about the crowds, the mania, the wrapping paper, and the unneeded stuff, I can focus on the spirit and beauty brought into this world by one unique birth.

Angels and Demons

We are programmed to categorize our experiences and our perceptions. There are so many stimuli coming at us each moment that if we didn't have some system of organization, we would be overwhelmed, frozen in place. An example would be: I see something. It has fur, four legs, and is alive. It fits into my category of animal. The tail is wagging, and it looks friendly, therefore it must be a dog. It is medium height, white, and has spots on it. It must be a Dalmatian. Since it looks friendly, I can pet it. This is our process to classify, creating neat little boxes of our experience.

However, past experience and stories can color our perception. One day I was told by the technician to leave a portable humidifier at his house for repair. I was to leave it in the open shed beside the house as he would not be there. I got out of the car and was retrieving the humidifier when an animal with four legs, big square head, and a nub of a tail bounded around the house. I knew immediately it was a pit bull dog. My first thought was to throw the humidifier at it and jump back in the car. However, it stopped and I saw the nub of the tail wag. It didn't bare its teeth. I placed the humidifier in the shed and, with some hesitation, stooped down and extended my hand. Much to my relief, I received a friendly lick. I was able to pet him and he was delirious with the attention. I had a prejudged image of a pit bull based on what I had heard and read. My prejudged image was all neatly ensconced in ordered categories.

How often do we do this with people? With one look, we immediately place them in preconceived categories. Even with all the stimuli coming

Musings

our way, it will benefit us and others to slow down long enough to look beyond the surface, feel the spirit, and connect with the soul.

I remember a story of *one* who did stop in the middle of the road, picking up a child and causing those around him to take notice, while his "staff" was trying to hurry him to a meeting.

Life has much beauty to behold. Sometimes we miss it because it was an unexpected wrapper that we cast into one of our categories without taking time to look deeper.

Think I will go out looking for some angels, instead of being too quick to make people into demons.

Moments

Lack of awareness of the moment is probably the state of being that holds us back more than anything else. We tend to live in our heads, dwelling on the ghosts of the past, reliving moments over and over. I call it "monkey brain," a lot of distracting chatter. If we can look at a past experience and learn from it, we can grow. However, to live in the past like Miss Havisham did in *Great Expectations*, still in her wedding dress from a wedding that never took place, is to be stuck, left behind, missing life. She even had all her clocks stopped at twenty minutes to nine.

When we live in "if only" this or that would happen, we are also stuck. Often, I dream of what my life would be if I won the lottery. (Of course, you have to buy a ticket first!) To be stuck in daydreaming is to miss life, although some planning helps give us direction.

"*Now*" is all we have. We really can't even count "now" in measurements, like seconds, because when we try to think about it, the next second has already gone to the following second. Being in the now is to be as aware of our surroundings, our feelings, our five senses as best we can.

I have always said the key to the best mental health is to be aware. Sometimes awareness comes with great struggle and pain. The nut has to crack to grow and become a tree. And the best way to rid ourselves of ghosts of the past is to face them head-on.

I think this nut will join Ghost Busters today!

It's A Mad, Mad, Mad, Mad World[6]

We cannot go through one day without feeling, facing, or hearing about anger. The newspaper is full of it. Anger and resulting violence has been a form of "entertainment" on television and in the movies ever since I can remember! Even Roy Rogers and Gene Autry dealt with it in facing guys in the black hats. However, we seem to have taken it to new levels in our society. I am not a "gamer" as in video games; however, I have seen some games and ads for games that have been jaw-dropping in their intense violence and disregard for mercy.

There have been sociological studies linking bullying and school violence with video games. We are gradually desensitizing a whole generation to violence. We are being taught that it is as common as brushing one's teeth.

I am no saint or prude, but I have some serious concerns about the concentration and focus our world seems to have on violent behavior. I have often wondered what news shows and newspapers would have to report if there were no violence or negative happenings going on in the world. Would there be news of celebration and success?

I am not naïve enough to think that we will eventually be able to reach a utopian society that no longer has anger and violence as a part of living. A fight or flight response to danger is programmed into our brain for survival. And yet, there are actions each of us can take not to drop any more rocks in the pond of turmoil we've already created.

One of the questions I ask myself when I encounter anger is, "What are they (or am I, for that matter) afraid of?" In every situation of anger I have encountered so far, I have been able to trace back to a specific fear. Take road rage, for instance. The person full of rage could be afraid of being harmed himself, of not being of value, or living a life of not being heard, or they could have had a fight with a wife or boss. Doesn't most anger have its foundation in fear?

Looking at it this way gives time not to react in kind. It also leads to compassion for the person with fear and a chance to control any triggers to our fight or flight response. Maybe this was what Jesus meant by telling us to love our enemies!

---

6. Kramer, "Mad World" *movie*.

Musings

Contagious Compassion

The secret to happiness is usually found in giving not getting. People who focus on themselves, making themselves secure, buying stuff for themselves have only fleeting happiness. When we take time to volunteer, to give of our time and presence to others, even if it is a small thing as a smile, sharing a seat, or offering to help someone lift a heavy item, we will feel better about life and ourselves. Perhaps we will live a bit longer.

Next time you are in a line at the drive-thru restaurant, pay for the person's food behind you. Drive off with a smile on your face. If we make a pledge to help one person each day for a month, we would probably be astounded at how contagious it would be, and how it reduces negativity. It could contribute to a groundswell toward world peace.

If we weren't so consumed with getting ahead and storing up treasures for ourselves, we might take time to reach out to others and be healthier and happier for it. Studies have been done showing when retired people volunteer, they live longer[7]. And this is probably true for all of us.

Our motivation for giving need not be to receive praise for our altruism. True giving is its own reward, when it comes from love and concern.

We have heard "survival of the fittest" keeps us alive. Maybe the "fittest" part is about being mature enough to help others survive. It gives us a sense of connection and meaning to the concept of "community."

Will Rodgers summarizes it well for me, "Too many people spend money they haven't earned to buy things they don't want, to impress people they don't like."[8]

Pack Time

Many days four o'clock finds one of us in the office on the computer. Abbie, our Shi Tzu, sits next to the chair and woofs periodically (a soft bark) until we get up and join the other one who is usually in the den. It's as if she is saying, "You have worked enough. Now it is time to stop and have pack time".

---

7. Harris and Thoresen, Psychology, 739–752.

8. Goodreads, Rodgers.

Musings

Dogs form packs. The dictionary describes a pack as "a group of domesticated animals who trained to hunt and run together."[9] Since my wife and I live in Abbie's house, she considers us her pack. If one of us is ill or not feeling well, she comes and lies next to us as if to make us feel better or protect us.

You may think I am stretching this interpretation of her behavior. I don't think so. There is a presence of spirit in her that goes beyond some genetic pattern born of a need for survival. "Could it be that these four-legged creatures are messengers of reason from God? "You work too much . . . it is time to rest." "You need to exercise daily . . . it is time to go for a walk." "You take life too seriously . . . it is time to play." "You don't feel good . . . let me be with you."

First thing each morning she comes running from the bedroom looking for me, dances on her hind feet to be picked up as if saying, "It's a new day, let's celebrate!"

For me, I am better for paying attention to this wee but obvious messenger for the need to play, rest, exercise, and have companionship when I'm feeling down. She reminds me that we have yet another day to be happy.

Time To Punt

When I was in college, we had a saying, "Drop back ten and punt." It is a football term for what a team has to do when their plans for reaching the goal line have been thwarted.

Today I had a list of "to dos" that would take me out of the house. I awoke and jumped out of bed to get started. (Well, I don't actually jump these days. It's more like slowly rolling out with popping sounds.) I looked out the window to a scene of blowing snow and an ice-covered driveway. There was nothing to do but "drop back ten and punt."

Part of living is shifting our goals from time to time. The winning attitude doesn't come from complaining about how we can't do what we envisioned. It comes from the excitement of a new adventure or project that we have been putting off. With snow and ice on the roads, twenty-seven degree temperatures, and winds at thirty-five miles per hour, consider building a fire in the fireplace or wood stove. Read a book and drink hot chocolate.

---

9. Merriam-Webster, "pack."

Musings

I think there should be a tenth beatitude that says, "Blessed are they whose plans have been foiled, for they shall be given the opportunity to see the world anew."

Have a great day . . . whatever it holds for you.

The Boot

I remember watching cartoons when I was a child. There was a scene where a character had rigged up a boot on some kind of contraption. He would back up to it, grab the rope hooked to it, and pull it. The boot would kick him in the seat of the pants every time he pulled the rope.

I hear people far too often pulling the self-kicking machine. I heard it frequently in my counseling practice. Actually, I don't know anyone who hasn't done it at times. I have. In the cartoon it looked pretty silly and it was meant to be. That was the kind of cartoons I grew up with . . . that would make me laugh at the absurdity of human behaviors. Need I mention Wily Coyote and the Road Runner, two of my favorites?

If it looks so silly and stupid, why do we do it? Why keep kicking ourselves when someone has already kicked us, and will continue if we allow it?

A person who would engage in such activity isn't valuing themselves at the moment, and yet, most of us do it from time to time. I could write all kinds of psychological speculation about low self-respect. An academic lecture we don't need.

Sometimes we are challenged in believing we have value. In the movie "The Help", there were several scenes where Aibileen Clark, the maid-nanny played by Viola Davis, would look directly into the eyes of the little girl and say, "You is kind. You is smart. You is important". Tears came to my eyes during these scenes. Many of us were never given such messages of love. Others of us never fully received the message someone with a loving intent was trying to impart.

Either way, we must learn to tell ourselves, "You is kind, You is smart, and You is important" enough times for it to reach our heart.

Give yourself a beautiful gift. Boot the boot!

And This Too Shall Pass

My dad used to say "And this too shall pass" when we were having a bad day or experiencing a difficult period of life. I never knew where he got the phrase. I always thought it was from the Bible, but could never find it. So I did some research and one source (footnote) says it originated with Persian Sufi poets, was said to be used by Edward Fitzgerald, an English poet, and quoted by Abraham Lincoln. It was also found in Jewish folklore.[10]

The is a story about a king who asked his wise men to create a ring that would make him happy when he was sad, and sad when he was happy. They created a ring with the words, "This too will pass." The king then realized both emotions are fleeting.[11]

"This too shall pass" is often offered as comfort when we have difficult times. Ups and downs are a part of being human. It's just the way life is. "This too will pass" is intended to give hope. In reality, whatever is happening will pass. We only have to look back on our own life and remember the difficult times and know that they did eventually go away. Or that we learned to accept or cope with them. Nothing remains the same. Change is constant. Most of us, when we are ill, feeling down, or in pain, wish that change would take place faster than it normally does!

So our pain and bad times as well as our joy and happiness will come and go. Accepting this reality is to endure the storms of life and accept that joy will come again.

I have always enjoyed thunder storms. (Call me weird.) There is something exciting about storms that are massive and powerful. I experience anticipation, awe, and fear. If we could find this kind of curiosity in the "storms" of our life, it may help us see that the things we don't like are passing, and calmer seas are ahead.

Patience and trust in a power greater than ourselves also help us accept that "this too shall pass."

Mine, All Mine!

The field of sociology makes a distinction between societies that honor cooperation, group effort, true democracy, and social equality, and societies that praise acts of "pulling yourself up by your boot straps," "standing above

---

10. Wikipedia, "pass."
11. Gerrold, *"Zen."*

Musings

the crowd," hero worship, etc. The first is classified as a collectivist society and the latter, an individualistic society.

Our country focuses a lot on the merits of the individual. We cover our walls and bookcases with diplomas, certificates, and trophies. We idolize individuals who stand out in the world of entertainment and feel like we are "somebody" when we can have our picture taken with them.

Many believe that our individual efforts entitle us to the trappings of success. So often in our journey to have it all, we pave the road with bodies we walked over getting there.

I think there is a gross paradox here. If we do it all ourselves and reach the top, there is only room for one. If we are able to have it all, that leaves a lot of people with less, maybe not enough to survive. It must be painful to walk that road alone and arrive at the top! Paul writes a whole chapter on our importance. The point of the chapter is made in one statement, "Now the body is not made up of one part but many." (I Corinthians 12)

The happiest people I have seen were a group sitting in broken-down sofas and chairs in a yard with no grass in front of a housing unit. The smiles and laughter were contagious. I could almost see an aura of warm light surrounding that group. And in my individualistic thinking, I wondered what in the world they had to be happy about.

I think I will go out looking for such a group and see if I can sit with them on a worn couch. Will they will make room for me?

Heaven on Earth

A number of years ago, I was fascinated by the television show *Northern Exposure*. I never missed an episode. The "church" in this series was "The Brick," a tavern in the center of town. People gathered to share, have fellowship, support one another, break bread, and have drink. They portrayed community, being part of something beyond the gathering of individuals.

Recently, I finished the British television series *Ballykissangel* about another small community. The neighborhood pub was called "Fitzgerald's". The local priest did a lot of his ministry at Fitzgerald's, hearing their stories and celebrating or easing the pain of their lives.

I am now reading the *Virgin River* novels, a series by the romance author Robyn Carr. (I am guilty as charged!) She paints a picture so vivid the reader is transported to the beautiful community of Virgin River. It is a community of people who love, go many an extra mile for each other and share what they have, creating a bond that leads to feelings of warmth and security.

If Jesus were to come again, I'm sure we would find him at The Brick, Fitzgerald's, and Jack's Bar in Virgin River. (The Bible describes him going to places and associating with people who defied the prevailing rules of the religious community.) Why are these fictitious places so attractive to me? No matter what happens in my life, I want to have people who care around me in my times of joy and need. "My" group also needs to be open to others seeking love and acceptance. The characters in many of my favorite novels and television series come with heavy baggage, but I see the people around them not being put off by it.

I will be revisiting *Northern Exposure*, renting the *Ballykissangel* DVDs, and reading Robyn Carr's series on Virgin River. They represent the possibility of how life could be if nothing else mattered but our relationships. They demonstrate how people find love, acceptance, and understanding. Where have you found a healthy affirming community?

The Ultimate Ride

Time is constantly moving forward. It doesn't stop. It doesn't start over. However, in our need to feel some control and organize the chaos around us, we compartmentalize a lot of life.

The beginning of a new year is often a time we make resolutions to change. With a fresh calendar we feel we can start anew. We can attempt to look and act better. I have even said to myself, "Beginning the first of the year, I will be more consistent with my exercise program and eat better." (It would have benefited me more to have thought of this during the "eating season" from Thanksgiving through Christmas!)

It is not bad to stop occasionally and review our lives, and decide if there are things we could work on in order to live better and with improved health.

However, there are often "devils" that cause us to struggle. Or maybe they are angels in disguise? Why does changing our lives for the better have to be so difficult? Isn't that what God challenges us to do throughout scripture? Often the cry inside my mind and body is, "Hey, I could use a little help here!"

Maybe life is about living each day, riding the waves of time. We can experience what comes our way during the day, make a difference in those

Musings

things we can change, observe the things we can't change, and hope for wisdom to know the difference between the two. Living with the chaos and the questions that seem to have no answers can bring internal peace. It often comes with hope and faith, and yes, Mr. Neibuhr[12], courage.

One old man on his death bed rose up, and his last words were, "Wow, what a ride!"

Climb aboard!

The Serenity Prayer

God grant me the serenity to accept the things I cannot change;
The courage to change the things I can;
And the wisdom to know the difference.[13]

No Mistakes

I have often heard people express the belief that if you aim your thoughts toward what you want, those things will happen. I have been skeptical of simplistic beliefs. In the movie *Field of Dreams*, that belief was its foundation, i.e., "If you build it, they will come."[14]

The more I think about it, the more the idea begins to make some sense. Our lives are greatly connected with the way we think and feel. However, if we just think hard enough about a new car, we most likely will not wake up to find it in our driveway the next morning. Yet, the thinking about it can guide us in the direction of working toward making that dream come true. We may cut back on some frivolous spending, put extra money into savings, and eventually be able to buy that car. There are bound to be a lot more benefits to positive thinking than to negative thoughts like, "It won't happen for me," "I'm never going to be able to do that," etc.

It is especially difficult to maintain dreams in the midst of pain, disappointment, and defeat. What does it do for us to stay stuck in this dark land of bleakness? I have often heard people say, "Don't be a Pollyanna." And I wonder, "Why not?" Pollyanna changed a whole community for the better with her unwavering optimism. It doesn't mean that we ignore the difficult and challenging experiences of life. We just use them to create something better. I have tried to live by this philosophy: "There are no mistakes, just

---

12. Niebuhr, *Essential Reinhold Niebuhr*.
13. Ibid., 251.
14. Robinson, *Field of Dreams*.

lessons". And, it seems a lot of my days are challenged by "lessons." I continue to be amazed at what I learn!

You are still in "school". What lessons are in store for you today?

Tough Atonement

I came home from school one day and my father was waiting. He said, "Sit down. I want to talk with you." Oh, boy! When my father wanted to talk, it usually meant I was in trouble. I got used to "the lecture," because my presumption usually came true. My Attention Deficit Hyperactive Disorder wasn't discovered during my childhood. I was classified as a creative and difficult child. If you know someone who has the disorder, or, better yet, if you live with that someone (just ask my wife), you know the kind of "outside-the-box" experiences that come with it.

Dad said, "I got a call from the mother of one of your classmates at school. Did you take the little girl's scarf and stomp it in the mud?" "We were just playing," I said. I got the lecture about the difference between "just playing" and being mean. I received a valuable lesson not only from the lecture but from having to enact a real life lesson on treating people with compassion and respect. Dad took me to the store, and I bought another scarf with my allowance. He drove me to her house and sat in the car as I walked up that long sidewalk, knocked on the door, gave her the new scarf, and apologized for my behavior. It was probably one of the most embarrassing and difficult moments of my life. Obviously, it left an impression (and a lesson!) as I am still talking about it.

At the time, I thought my dad was being unduly hard on me. I did not know I was wrong at the time. At that age, my classmates and I always teased girls. The scarf fell in the mud puddle as I grabbed it to run and play "keep away."

As I look back on it, and I have many times, I am truly thankful that my father took the time to teach me a moral code and a compassion for others. When I went to bed that night, I felt lightness in my heart.

To have the courage to clean up messes we have made, apologize to people we have hurt, and deal with baggage that weighs us down fills us with an incredible sense of freedom. It may be difficult and embarrassing. Those we ask for forgiveness may not respond with kindness. However, we can have a cleansing experience, no matter what happens after the apology.

Musings

May we have the courage to admit our hurtful behaviors, and clean them up with our actions. May your year be filled with less baggage and a lightness of heart.

Trading Places

We live in a world of wars, of violence brought about by strongly-held religious and secular beliefs and by loyalty to certain groups. We have "mini-wars" in sports, although no war is small. All you have to do to see the today's zealots is to attend a college or professional football game. Tragically, such zeal has escalated to murder in the parking lot. I saw this ill-directed zeal coaching Little League when I had to threaten a father with being asked to leave practice for ranting at his visibly shaken ten-year-old.

Where wars and differing religious beliefs are concerned, if we could set aside our beliefs long enough to really listen to someone's beliefs and respect their passion, we might gain understanding and compassion. Even better, if we could live with that person for a week or a month, a whole new world could open up for us.

I don't believe the common people really hate other races, countries or religions. Hate is an emotion and way of relating that is taught or conditioned in us by role models. There is a power in charismatic leadership that "hypnotizes" the masses into frenzied prejudice toward those who are different. We only have to look as far as Hitler.

What would it be like to live with a family in Afghanistan or Iran for an extended period and learn their language and rituals? Or what fun it would be to have some good-hearted wagering between opposing fans, like a University of Georgia fan wagering a case of peaches against a case of oranges with the Florida Gators!

When did "civility" and respect for our differences get diminished or lost along the way?

Choices

We often hear statements like: "He made me angry." "You make me want to tear my hair out." "She made me want to scream." It is like we are walking around with buttons that people can see. All they have to do reach out and push one. We often react without thinking. Those "buttons" are called wounds. It hurts when someone does or says something to remind us of those wounds.

When I was leading seminars, I argued that no one can "make" you do or think anything. Any time we use the above "reactionary" statements, we are giving people power over us. You say, "Come on! If someone slaps you across the face, don't tell me you aren't going to get angry?" If you look at anger's source, fear is often at its core. Science describes our "fight or flight" response. When threatened, we can fight or we can run. That still gives us the power of choice, doesn't it? Maybe there is a third choice-- finding "the peace that passes all understanding." (Phil 4:7)

Mahatma Gandhi is a great example for the power of personal choice. I remember the scene in the movie where Ben Kingsley, playing Gandhi, was hit across the forearm with a Billy club by an English bobby. Gandhi just looked into the face of the officer with tears of pain but also with compassion. The power of Gandhi claimed in choosing his reaction played a part in the British government allowing India its independence.

It takes a great deal of self-control and a feeling of self-worth not to react immediately, but to choose a more productive response.

During meditation and reflection before we face conflict, we can envision the choices we have and consider the peace-giving ones. When confrontation comes, we may be more conscious of having a choice.

I invite you to practice creating responses of peace. We are not passive slaves to our reactions. We have the power to be masters of our responses. It takes practice and patience to respond out of that place of peace.

I am still in training, and probably will be for the rest of my life.

Alive or Dead

Funeral homes turn me off, especially the employee dress code: black suits, starched white shirts, and high-glossed shoes, all so immaculately tailored. Even a pastel shirt would ease the stiffness. I took a tour of a funeral home once for a class on death and dying. We were escorted back to see the caskets. As I walked through the door, on both sides were the most expensive caskets, displayed on pedestals with lights, curtains, and potted plants. The farther I went back into the room, both the displays and the caskets were obviously less expensive, inviting the label "inferior" by comparison. In the back with almost no light was a simple pine box with a thin outer coating designed to look like felt or cloth. This experience reminded me of the car

Musings

dealership I worked at one summer where cars were the merchandise on display. (I have a vivid and sometimes unwieldy imagination.)

I attended the funeral of one of my wife's cousins. The cousin lying in the casket wasn't there. There was just so much physical matter. You have heard people say, "Doesn't *it* look so much like him?" Unknowingly they were attesting to the fact that no one was there inside the body.

I was suddenly struck that he WAS there. There was an incredible energy in the room—a buzz of conversation and laughter that went beyond just the sharing of memories, perhaps inspired by the ongoing slide show. This room was not permeated with death and solemn air. There was a party going on and he shared it with us.

As Paul said, "Just as the body, though one, has many parts, but all of its parts form one body . . . . "(1 Cor 12: 12) Maybe this is just another sign of life beyond death. We were certainly connected, those of us living, and the one who had just left his body!

"Skin On"

What do you do when the pain of living gets so intense that you have no strength left to deal with life? We are taught that we can turn our cares, wounds, and hurts over to God. However, I am like the little boy in his room who was terrified of a thunderstorm. When his mother came in to see what he was upset about, she sat on his bed and said, "Don't you know that God will take care of you?" He responded, "Yes, but I want someone with *skin on.*"

We don't have to deal with the challenges of life by ourselves. There is a theological term called "incarnation," which means God is within us, not a distant being observing our life. It is always interesting to me when people point upward when referring to God. I guess that comes from associating heaven with that which is above us. (When you think about it, once you get beyond earth's atmosphere, there is no up, down, or sideways!)

Incarnation (God in the "flesh") presupposes that God is present "with skin on." Reaching out to others when life gets overwhelming can give us relief and comfort. We see this being done successfully in twelve step programs like AA, Al-Anon and EA.

I remember when I was a child, in my dad's churches people periodically stood up to give their "testimonies". These weren't always a confession of their conversion or belief in God, but a vulnerable plea for prayer and for help for a crisis in their lives. They were reaching out to "God incarnate" and their community for love and support in their pain and confusion. We have gotten so used to putting on "Sunday-go-to-meeting clothes" that we often cover our pain and need for support even when we are in community.

Maybe we are seeing the value of support from someone with "skin on". Small groups are being created (Stephen Ministries, Grief Workshops, and twelve-step programs) to provide a place for "soothing of the wounded soul."

Like the ad for Bell Telephone Company says, "Reach out and touch someone."

We Know

How many times have we come to a point in life where we have to make a decision between two choices, and on the surface they seem equally acceptable or difficult? Internally we agonize: "What should I do? " "God, please help me make a decision." Or we ask others, "What would you do?" Some will tell us what to do, and the risk is that they get angry if we don't follow their advice. Or we take the risk of anger if we take their advice and it doesn't work out.

We are often challenged with difficult decisions. Life is like that. You could say that it is one of the gifts God has given us. How can making an agonizing decision be a gift? First, it reminds us of the gift of our freedom. Second, it says God believes you have what it takes to make a right decision. And finally, making those kinds of decisions helps us develop self-worth and inner strength.

The hurry and complexity of our society make these kinds of decisions more difficult. In a fast-paced world full of stimuli, there seems to be no room to think clearly, to be calm enough to process the direction and consequences of each choice.

My father used to say, "Listen to the still small voice within." (I Kings 19:12 KJV) We have to take time to be still and listen to hear that voice. There is a voice within, and we know the direction to take even before the struggle. Often times, the voice tells us to take the more difficult choice.

It is said best in one of my favorite poems. I can't say it better so I will reprint it here:

Musings

The Road Not Taken

Two roads diverged in a yellow wood,
And sorry I could not travel both
And be one traveler, long I stood
And looked down one as far as I could
To where it bent in the undergrowth;

Then the other, just as fair,
And having perhaps the better claim,
Because it was grassy and wanted wear;
Though as far that the passing there
Had worn then really about the same,

And both that morning equally lay
In leaves no step had trodden black
Oh, I kept the first for another day!
Yet knowing how way leads on to way,
I doubted if I should ever come back.

I shall be telling this with a sigh
Somewhere ages and ages hence:
Two roads diverged in a wood, and I—
I took the one less traveled by
And that has made all the difference.

—Robert Frost (1874 to 1963), *Mountain Interval*, 1920.[15]

You Are Me. I Am You.

Physically we are not the same persons we were two years ago. Science shows us all of our cells, molecules, and chemistry change about every two years. We keep producing the elements that constitute our physical bodies as we go about our daily routines of eating and drinking. The old bodily material gets sloughed off and eliminated to be recycled by the earth.

---

15 Lathem, *Frost*, 105.

When we think about it, we are actually sharing our base materials with each other. The air we breathe has been breathed by others for centuries. Air is made of nitrogen and oxygen and a few other trace elements. These elements have been floating around in and out of lungs for centuries. As weird as it sounds, components of cells that were in someone else's body are the material that is making new cells in our bodies. The air we have in our lungs once was in the lungs of others. One could say this is scientific proof of what has been said in the Bible about us being one body. Paul says, " . . . for we are all members of one body." (Eph. 25b)

We are not only our brother's and sister's keepers, we are our brother and sister—red, yellow, black, white, Christian, Hindu, Buddhist, Muslim, and many others. If we remember this the next time we look at someone else, we may move toward them with more compassion and harmony. I love what John A. (Slow Turtle "Cjegktoonuppai") Peters of the Wampanoag Indian Tribe says, "It is said, 'Love thy neighbor as thyself.' That is the trouble, most of us do."[16]

What he is saying here is that most of us really haven't learned the measuring part, to love ourselves. Therefore, we often treat others with contempt because we haven't learned to love ourselves.

The times I am really content with myself (and they aren't frequent enough), I am able to have a lot more tolerance and compassion for others.

I'm still a work in progress. You too?

Things

Why we are driven to have new and more things? What is missing in our lives that we try to fill it with "stuff"? The same question may be asked when we overdo it with "comfort food." There is nothing wrong with nurturing ourselves with comfort food in times of crisis. Yet when we are trying to fill a bottomless hole in our spirits with things and food (or anything else that could be called an obsession or addiction), we are doomed to failure.

It takes real courage and maybe even professional guidance to look at what is a very painful wound. I do think at some level we know something is missing from our lives. We are pros at rationalizing our "hunting and gathering" activities. We have even made accumulating the newest and best a sign of success. We all have seen the bumper sticker that says, "The one who dies with the most toys wins."

16. Peters, *"Great Spirit.God,"* Facebook.com

Musings

Frederick Buechner, in his book *Whispering in the Dark*, makes this painfully true statement, "There are people who use up their entire lives making money so they can enjoy the lives they have entirely used up."[17] How profound!

Jesus also spoke to this misguided focus in our lives when he mentioned the futility of storing up treasures (Matt 6:19–20), or drinking from a well that will not satisfy your thirst. (John 4: 1–26) When we hear on Sunday morning, "This is the bread of life, this is the cup of salvation," can we transcend the moment and go to a place of spiritual fulfillment and joy, where nothing matters except to be one with all of life? Or do we just go through the motions while thinking about something totally outside the moment? We have to think about and practice good habits to be immersed in a new way of being.

I have to work at being present. When I succeed at being present, I am more relaxed, content and fulfilled.

Too Little Time

It seems this lifetime isn't long enough for me to experience all that I would like to experience. My bucket list seems to be endless. I continue to be excited by discovering new things in life, even when I discover a new word. The word "atavism" appeared in my current novel. Fascinated by a new word, I looked up the definition. Atavism is defined as, "The reappearance of a characteristic in an organism, usually caused by the chance recombination of genes."[18] For me, it's like finding an elephant with fur or hair from its mastodon ancestors. Well, I am not giving a study of etymology here, just giving an example of how little we know. I love life and feel like I'm still a little boy with bugs and frogs in his pockets.

Every day can be like Christmas with a new package to unwrap. Sometimes we have to work at slowing down long enough to be awed by what's around us. New discoveries fill us with excitement, joy, and happiness. If we look at all experiences as positive, then even what we call mistakes become lessons, something new to be learned.

This inspires me to ask a question and fantasize about possibilities. Where do all the spirits come from that make us persons? How many souls would there be if each person who has lived from the beginning of human

17. Buechner, *Whistling*, 80.
18. The Free Dictionary, "atavism."

life still existed? Is each baby born a new individual creation with a soul that has never been before?

I like to think we have a choice as to whether we can experience another finite life. Look at the amount of wisdom and experience a soul could have accumulated in another life. For instance, if you are a male, there is no way to truly know what it is like to be a female, or for a Caucasian to be an African American, or for an accountant to be a rock star, etc. I may be part Hindu, a person who believes in reincarnation and returning to earth in a different body. If God can be incarnate in us and we are created in God's image, then future incarnations might be possible. We sometimes meet a person, usually younger, that we sense is an old soul, someone who embodies the wisdom of other lifetimes.

After a much-deserved rest, I would like to try it again. It has been fascinating to this point, even with the painful challenges. Sitting on a cloud playing a harp for eternity doesn't sound very appealing to my restless spirit. Worse yet, it sounds downright boring. Maybe it's my next lesson.

Sands of Time

Yesterday, I wrote about Too Little Time. The more I think about it, the more I question how we handle the time we have been given.

We are called human beings, and yet, we spend most of our time doing! For some, the reason for constant activity comes from trying to please others, and fill the hole of feeling unloved, inferior, or unworthy. For others, constant activity is focused on achieving "The American Dream." That has meant climbing over as many people as one thinks is necessary to get to the top. We have justified this behavior by calling it "becoming successful." For some, busyness is a continuous filling of all the spaces so we don't have to face our own mortality. Often the drive and desire to experience as much as possible can cause us to miss the awareness and essence of the moment. When our lives become a "blurrr" of running from one to the next chore, task, or item on the "to do" list, we miss the peace and beauty of the moment. Moments are all we have. The popular soap opera, *Days of our Lives*, opens with the words, "like sands through an hour glass, so are the days of our lives."

Maybe we have it backwards! Could it be that if we slow down, we will experience *more* of life?

I've made an observation in traffic. I sometimes see someone driving fast, passing cars at every chance, and obviously in a snit to get somewhere in the least possible time. On the other hand, I am driving at a normal speed, not passing or rushing. I come to a stop light. I look over and see that person who zoomed by me ten miles back sitting in the other lane, not having made any better time than me. (At times I have also been that other driver!)

I do feel more like a human *being* after time spent in contemplation. Some of us have become minimalists in our accumulation. Maybe we can also become minimalists in our doing. God encourages us to take time to watch the lilies in the field. (Matt 6:30)

A friend of mine says there are Ten Commandments and only nine beatitudes, so why not create another beatitude, something like this "blessed are those who slow down, for they shall see the world in a grain of sand"?

Maybe that's why we go to the beach.

Where is Happiness?

I listen to people talk about their desires. The one thing that I hear most often is, "I just want to be happy!" Who doesn't want to live a life full of joy, a life of feeling up, in a constant state of satisfaction?

I have a question. If we were born happy and never experienced sadness, grief, feeling down, etc., how would we know what feeling happy was like?

Life is full of contrasts. The Chinese refer to the yin and yang of life, ☯ the negative and the positive. Experiencing the negative or down side of living allows us to appreciate the positive side in living.

Happiness is fleeting. We may experience moments, or even longer blocks of time feeling joyful and satisfied. Then we come back to the everyday business of life.

We can strive for situations and experiences that give us happiness. They may be different for each person, such as time at the beach, reading a book that lifts us up, digging in the garden or celebrating with friends. The list goes on. Be aware that each of these times will have an ending.

Although happiness is a desirable endeavor, a more reasonable striving is to be content. I like Webster's definition for content: "pleased and satisfied: not needing more."[19] This is the ability to accept life as it comes,

---

19. Merriam-Webster, "content."

allowing each moment to be an experience of what it is. I often use the expression "living life, accepting what's so". If we reach this state of being, we are content. We can look at experience with curiosity. You say, "How can you be content with suffering or other difficulties of living?" The Buddhist philosophy is that if you accept that life is difficult, you can transcend it; it is no longer difficult, because it no longer matters. It is just part of the package.

Jesus also speaks to those in distress: Blessed are the poor in spirit . . . ; Blessed are the meek . . . ; Blessed are those who mourn . . . . ; Blessed are those who hunger and thirst . . . ; Blessed are those who are persecuted . . . (Matt 5:1–12) Could this be an invitation to contentment?

Most of us spend time resisting the loss of happiness. We don't see that the resisting is taking our energy and robbing us of contentment. Can you imagine being able to say to some "curve ball" that comes our way, "Oh, this is interesting. I wonder what I can learn from this?"

Believe me, I am still learning. Contentment is a journey.

The Listening Heart

People are naturally drawn to each other when they are out in public, especially at an event. We gather in groups to share beliefs, ideas, and experiences. There is no doubt we are social creatures. Unfortunately, we too often engage in what is called "walking over each other." We interrupt while someone is talking, or we jump in and say, "You think that is something? Let tell you about this." Groups also seem to get louder the longer they meet as people try to be sure they are heard? We think we are right and others ought to listen. I started to say it happens mostly with my gender, but my wife informs me that she also experiences women engaging in a battle of words. And it is just "words." The spirit and feeling that we have not been heard, along with feeling empty, is the end result.

Do we really listen? To really hear, one has to shut down one's thoughts and focus on what the other person is saying. That gives us the ability to really hear them. It is not just the vibration of vocal cords meeting the vibration of ear drums that is happening. Listening involves deep feelings and a spiritual side of communication as well. To hear another is to encompass the other person with love and attend to their whole being. This is difficult and takes some concentration. We have to work at shutting down the chatter in our own minds (monkey minds), and quit trying to formulate what we think are more intelligent responses.

Was Jesus referring to this when he said, "Who has ears let him hear. To what can I compare this generation? They are like children sitting in the market places and calling out to others." (Matt 11:15–16) "For this people's hearts have been calloused; they hardly hear with their ears, and have closed their eyes. Otherwise, they might see with their eyes, hear with their ears, *understand with their hearts*, and turn and I would heal them." (Matt 13:15)

I have noticed when someone in a group doesn't say anything. Or if there is an opening or lull in the conversation, he or she will say something that causes all others to stop and look as if they have just heard something profound. The speaker is usually older and the lines in his/her face speak of wisdom.

I guess this is why I am drawn to the old Zen masters in movies. There is something peaceful, graceful, and knowing about their presence.

As I get older, I find myself listening more. I don't know whether I have less energy to fight a battle of words, or whether I have gained some wisdom about real listening.

What will you hear today that will fill you with grace?

To See or Not to See

> Blinded by our limited seeing,
> we walk this journey as did Thomas.
> These rods and cones create the illusion
> that light rays before us are the only reality.
> We are as flies on the ceiling of the Sistine Chapel,
> unaware of the gods that float all around us.
> Doomed to the certitude of our physical perception,
> we miss worlds just beyond our aimless wandering.
>
> We must release our fierce grip on physical conviction
> in order to transcend the curtains just beside us.
> To let go of such conditioned assuredness
> is to fly to new worlds of awareness.
> Once we leap to be supported by the substance of our souls
> (or angels unaware),

> we find a new security that never fails us.
> Our solid foundation is then secured
> as we reconnect to our sacred oneness.

—Edward L. Boye, 2000

Identity Crisis

In the world of self-help books and growth seminars, we are told to be ourselves, be who we are, and be true to our real self. This may a challenging task. How do I get clarity about who is the *real* me? People spend years in therapy trying to figure it out.

To begin with, we must understand what society, tradition, and caretakers have ingrained in us. We were dependent for so long on these significant others that their word has great impact on how we see ourselves and life. We want to be accepted and to fit in, we allow what is expected of us to control our lives.

Finding the real person at the core of our being takes some patient self-reflection. One way to do this is by sorting through what we are doing to please others, and what we know and feel in our gut. When we stop to think and feel, we know. The truth is right there at our core.

The challenge, then, is to have the courage to manifest those feelings, and not be controlled by the expectations outside of us. This takes a certain inner strength, a trust in oneself, and faith in a power beyond our own being. This doesn't mean that you always do your own thing but it does mean you are conscious in making a choice to either follow others or to march to a different beat.

Being true and honest to *you* is a risk. We have to risk not being liked for our choices. Jesus challenged us to think independently, "Why don't you judge for yourselves what is right?" (Luke 12:57). And later, Paul says, "Each one should test his own actions. Then he can take pride in himself . . . for each one should carry his own load". (Gal 6:4–5) What is the "load" he is talking about? Part of my load is figuring out who I am, and being as honest about that as possible. Those who are not secure with themselves are motivated by fear to coerce, manipulate, seduce, and control those around them trying to feel secure, but end up feeling empty.

The only way to feel secure is to feel an inner peace that allows us "to boldly go where no man [or woman] has gone before." (*Star Trek*

TV introduction) This can take us to a place where we have to live with uncertainty.

Scott Peck, in his bestselling book, *The Road Less Traveled*, says, "The path to holiness lies in questioning everything."[20] Being true to the real you is to be in a holy place. And if you are the real you, you can allow others to be who they are. You don't need for others to be a certain way for you to be okay.

Hey, if you feel like dancing in the street, go for it!

Feet of Clay

We like to feel powerful-- to feel strong physically; to make choices without fear; to be respected as individuals who have authority and influence; to take on the challenges of life; to be able to stand above the crowd. Unfortunately, most of us define power as being able to apply coercive, external force or pressure; to be in control; to dominate. Domination does not bring about transformation or peace; it is control fueled by fear. Domination is about moving things around. It blocks transformation. It is the basis of all wars. Its end result is separation, isolation, and loneliness.

There is another kind of power that is a selfless power, a sharing power, a benevolent use of power that comes from within. People can be transformed by the spirit of another person. Those who have developed this kind of power seem to move through life with a calm, compassionate demeanor. They attract rather than repel others. This power comes from being able to love and accept oneself. When we incorporate this kind of power, there is no longer any need or desire to see the other person as different or wrong. We discover that we are more tolerant of others when we are content with who we are.

In our society external success, material possessions, and outside recognition have been placed upon a pedestal. We claim, "My team is better," "My beliefs are the right ones." "He knows the right people." "She can pull the right strings." The term "tin gods with clay feet" was often used in my counseling training. (This comes from a dream that King Nebuchadnezzar had of a huge statue made of precious metals with clay feet. Daniel interpreted the dream to mean that the kingdom would fall. (Dan 2) Today we see people who stand out above the crowd--- entertainers, politicians, ministers, and other public figures who have obtained this kind of power

---

20. Peck, *The Road Less Traveled*, 194.

and status by force. Can we not find more people worth imitating than those with an intense negative drive to come out on top politically or socially?

We become tin gods but forget our feet of clay when we ignore our vulnerability. We can't live on that pedestal without eventually falling, shattering those clay feet and feeling our bodies dented and rusting. Just ask Jimmy Swaggart, Jim Baker, Richard Nixon, Elvis Presley, Michael Jackson, etc. I think sometimes the isolation and desperation that comes from being on that fragile pedestal makes us unconsciously engage in acts that show our humanness. To be truly human is to be vulnerable, to have some "warts."

Power from within, based on a healthy sense of self with an element of humility is more effective in creating lasting change, though transformation may take place more slowly. A willingness to have faith and patience is crucial for this nonviolent and compassionate power to endure. I have mentioned Gandhi, Martin Luther King Jr and, yes, Jesus as having this kind of power.

When we take time to listen to others and accept them as they are, we encourage them to be open to new ideas. Power comes through humility but we don't commonly look at it this way. Let us never forget our feet of clay molded by the Master Potter's hands.

Beside Oneself

"I want more." "I wish I could be like him or her." "If only I could win the lottery, life would be great." These statements reflect standing apart from oneself, looking for something to bring contentment. If we are beside ourselves, we are split apart and can't see clearly. We were not made to live outside of who we really are. Reality only resides in the now. Flying from west to east often means it will take a couple of days for your spirit to catch up with your body. One feels out of sorts. Science says that our circadian rhythm (internal clock) is out of balance.

Projecting our self, our soul, our being to somewhere besides right now prevents us from seeing the beauty and the mystery of life as it happens. Wanting to be someone else doesn't allow us to see how unique and beautiful we are. If we spend our time wishing we were like someone else or wanting to be somewhere besides where we are, it is like we are suffering from a nonclinical form of "multiple personalities", an escape from our real self.

Maybe Jesus was telling us how not to be split when he said, "You are the light of the world . . . let your light shine before others." (Matt 5:14–16)

Musings

It is futile to want to live someone else's life. Jesus also said, "Do not store up treasures on earth." (Matt 6:19) Focusing on these "treasures" also takes us out of our true selves. Besides, you might end up on the television series, *The Hoarders*.

If we could have it all or change places with someone else, we would have missed the gift of being ourselves.

My dad used to tell a story from the pulpit that seemed absurd. A high-powered businessman who worked all the time to get to the top of his profession came out of his office building one day. He stopped to buy a newspaper from a boy selling them on the corner. The man was impressed with the young man's hard-working approach. He said, "Young man, where did you learn to be so industrious?" The boy said in surprise, "Why, Dad!" There are those who never know their own children or anyone else because they live outside themselves. They have eyes but they do not see. They are "beside themselves".

I like me, "warts" and all. Will you say the same about you?

Living Mirror

"O wad some Power the giftie gie us
To see oursels as ithers see us!"[21]

This is an often quoted phrase from Robert Burns, the Scottish poet. "Oh, would some Power the gift give us, to see ourselves as others see us!" Would it be a gift for us to be able to see ourselves through the eyes and thoughts of others? I guess it depends on who the others are and what we are doing at the time!

We have an opportunity to begin to get a sense of what others think, see, and feel about us. We cannot get into their brains and see through their eyes, but we can observe them and their physical reactions and messages. We can connect with their spirits and their energy as they speak to us.

This is not as easy as it sounds. When we encounter another person, our "monkey minds" are often on turbo speed. Thoughts begin churning in our heads: "I wonder what they are thinking?" "Do I have spinach in my teeth?" "Is my fly open?" "Is my bra strap showing?" With all this mental chatter, it is no wonder we can't connect to the quiet messages that are coming our way.

21. Burns, *To A Louse*.

The other day someone gave me a compliment about myself that I really had not accepted or thought about in a positive way. I did stop, look at them, and not only heard their words but felt their sincerity, warmth and a connection of our souls. I felt affirmed, seeing myself from a different perspective.

Not everything others say about us will make us feel good immediately. There may be constructive criticism that is initially hard to take but still helps us grow. In the end, we must be strong enough to discern what is valuable.

In order to "see oursels as ithers see us," we must be willing to stop our mind static, be in the moment, be open to receive, and draw the other person into our souls.

We are creatures of community. We need to be able to give and to receive from those with whom we commune. The most difficult of these is to receive.

Practice seeing yourself through someone else's eyes. You might be surprised by their gifts to you!

Unlikely Angels

Why do we find it hard to accept that change often depends on our giving up things that have been ingrained in us by others who are certain how things ought to be? In our loneliness, insecurity and desperation to be accepted, we are too often swayed by comments like: "This is the way it is done" or "We have always done it this way." Do we march to the beat of the crowd, or do we go with what we know in our souls is more loving and creative, even though it's a little uncomfortable? I'm not suggesting always marching to our own beat when we're feeling rebellious or "cutting our nose off to spite our face," but that we consider a different path when the situation calls for creativity, love, and inclusiveness.

Where do we find the road paved with inspiration? Sometimes it is in the most unlikely places, in people we most often discount. We become complacent and are blinded by relying on stereotypical labels.

It seems that those who stand out in the Bible are the ones who went outside the system. Sarah was barren until a miracle allowed her to conceive; the prodigal son was accepted into his father's house after he wasted his inheritance; John the Baptist preached in the wilderness; Mary, a humble maiden was betrothed to Joseph the carpenter; and Jesus was the son of Mary. In modern history, we have Abraham Lincoln who was born in a frontier cabin; Martin Luther King Jr., the son of a southern African-American preacher during segregation; and Rosa Parks, an African-American department store clerk who wouldn't give up her seat to a white person on a crowded bus . . . I could name many others. All came from humble beginnings. All were unknowns, common people at the bottom of life's hierarchy. And yet, they all made major contributions that made the world a better place.

Maybe we ought to listen more closely to the janitor, the cashier, the homeless person. They have experienced more than many have in two lifetimes.

My most shocking revelation came from a mental patient in the hospital where I did my internship. She looked at me one day and said, "You look like you ought to be in here with us." I was shocked to say the least. When the ground felt somewhat solid again, I thought, "Hey, I am the one trying to help you put your life back together. What could you possibly mean?" When I let go of my arrogance and fear, I realized that I was feeling depressed and "wandering in the darkness" that day, and on other days as well. How perceptive and honest she was with me. Who would know any better than someone in the throes of mental struggle? She gave me cause to do some soul searching.

Don't discount someone because they are not in a position of authority, well known, a member of an exclusive club or in a place of status in life.

You may be "entertaining angels unaware."

Old Souls

From time to time, we hear people say that someone is an "old soul." This observation refers to people who have a deeper sense of life, who see beyond the moment and have more wisdom than we expect. Although "old souls" span all ages, these people are usually younger than someone who would have that kind of insight.

Old souls seem to live more in the world of spiritual "knowing and seeing." That kind of knowing goes beyond mental knowledge. Not only do they seem to have a clearer understanding of reality, but also an awareness of other worlds.

Many of us see glimpses of what is beyond the physical world around us. It is like we live next to a curtain, and occasionally we get to briefly stick our head through this curtain and see to the other side. It is an "ah-ha" experience. It is a moment of wonder, hope, excitement, and comfort. Maybe the word grace is part of this experience. I like M. Scott Peck's definition of grace: " . . . a powerful force originating outside of human consciousness which nurtures the spiritual growth of human beings."[22] Maybe it means seeing a glimpse of heaven. The words spoken from these "old souls" have an element of the divine; their words are spoken from their hearts and transcend normal living.

As I have often said, listening doesn't come easy. It pays to be open to everyone. The hard work comes in sorting through what is said to find what is meaningful and valuable.

Once on a camping trip out west, a group of Boy Scouts and I panned for gold. I took my first pan out of the water and excitedly told our guide, "Man, this is easy. There are gold flakes all though this sand." He smiled and said, "You have to learn the difference between fool's gold (pyrite) and real gold. There is always more fool's gold than real gold." It takes a discerning eye to discover real gold. After several hours, I had discovered one flake of real gold!

Finding the "gold" in what we hear is very similar. Those "old souls" usually don't have a lot to say, but what they do say is often pure gold.

Images

    The soft, warm smells of a sunny day
    Transport my being to summertime long ago.
    A curious child on my grandmother's farm
    Lying on a hill watching clouds form celestial images,
    Feeding an imagination already rich with worlds not seen.

    The dry hay rich with golden warmth,
    Sweet clover crushed releasing the rich herbal aroma,
    Cool aqueous waves of the nearby pond,
    The scent of budding fruit from grandfather's orchard,

---

22. Peck, *The Road Less Traveled*, 261.

Musings

> These memories so real that I am there again—
> Feeling the grass, rustling hay, and spitting seeds through the limbs of the cherry tree.
> Yes, our spirits do transcend these physical bonds.
> How glorious a gift from our loving Creator!

—Edward L. Boye, 2008

Chaos

We live in a chaotic, uncertain world. Most of us feel insecure, not knowing what is going to happen next. We spend a lot of time and energy seeking answers and struggle to create order out of chaos. We are uncomfortable with extremes and the unknown.

Many try to explain the teachings of the Bible coming from a place of fear and insecurity. We often think structure will relieve our uncertainty. Have you noticed we have a variety of often conflicting church doctrines proclaimed as truth? The more we put our trust in one specific doctrine, the more we thirst for more structure.

How can we have a sense of peace in this chaotic world? It takes great faith, personal internal trust and a sound sense of self. Once we accept that life is living with the questions and having loose ends floating around, chaos is no longer an issue. Trusting that we will be all right in the midst of the chaos is the ultimate act of faith.

Most of us think we want to be in the middle of the balancing scale with no ups or downs. As children, see-saws terrified and thrilled us. I believe the thrill is the soul wanting to be at home in the chaos. Once challenges and unanswered questions are accepted, fear can become an exciting adventure.

The Bible is a book of chaos and questions. It tells us that life is chaotic, unfair, and at times brutal. The ultimate answer is a paradox. Accept the uncertainty of it all, and then have faith.

An old woman and man lived in a cabin on the back side of a mountain. They didn't get much news. A new road was being built on the other side of their mountain. One day the road crew started dynamiting. The cabin shook, pots and pans began to fall on the floor, and the windows rattled. The old woman came running out onto the front porch where the man was sitting in a rocking chair smoking his pipe. She said "Caleb, the

Lord is destroying the world." He kept rocking, smoking his pipe, looking out over the beautiful vista. Then he said, "Well, hit's his'n, ain't it?"

That's the way I want to live. How about you?

Sacred Dirt

The earth is often called a ball of dirt floating in space. Scientists say it is made up of rocks, soil, water, and gas. We perceive there is a separation between the mineral world and the living (animal or vegetable) world. Our perception has given us the emotional distance needed to use earth's materials without considering the effects of our actions. To rob or take by force for one's own satisfaction without regard for consequences is akin to rape. Are we raping, plundering the earth for all it can give without compassion for its being alive?

We have been told that we have an interconnected ecological system; if one species fails, it affects the whole structure.

I drive along the state highway near my home and see an almost constant trail of plastic bags, cups, cans, bottles, diapers, cigarette butts, etc. This next example is most painful to me. I go back to the Appalachian Mountains I call home and see mountain tops literally being cut off, with the dirt and rock pushed over the edge to fill the streams. All done to gouge out the coal. All one has to do is fly over the area to see the desecration.

Maybe, just maybe, if we saw every part of the earth that we call mineral, inanimate objects as part of the living earth, we might act with respect. A sense of awe of the beauty of life can fill us with more humility. We may not be the ones cutting off the mountain tops. We do have the power to stop it (that is, if our representatives will listen to us). It takes time and numbers to put pressure on our government officials to make the changes needed to protect the environment. We can also make sure we live our lives as if everything is sacred. The Psalms and other parts of the Bible are full of the sacredness and beauty of the earth. To be given dominion does not translate into permission to destroy.

Yes, you can call me a "tree-hugging, bleeding heart," or you can call me a child of God who has been given the honor and responsibility of taking care of this gift that sustains us.

I think I will go out and pick up some trash.

Musings

Life is Difficult

Life is difficult. I don't have to tell you that. Being able to see it on paper reminds us that this journey is challenging. I have read many quotes about suffering, and a lot of them say that suffering is part of being alive. Elbert Hubbard, American editor and writer (1856 to 1915) said, "If you suffer, thank God!— it is a sure sign that you are alive."[23] It's like the statement "It is better than the alternative." For some, I am not so sure.

Learning to accept suffering is one of the four noble truths of Buddhism. Buddhists believe that if we accept that suffering is part of life, it ceases to be suffering. In a way they are saying, "Don't resist it, but accept it and then it just becomes part of life."

The Bible frequently mentions suffering. In Matthew, Jesus states, "Blessed are they that mourn for they will be comforted." (Matt 5:4) In Romans we read " . . . we also glory in our sufferings because we know that suffering produces perseverance; perseverance, character; and character, hope." (Rom. 5:3-4) How can we feel blessed, happy, or joyful when we are hurting? There are days we have a difficult time accepting physical and emotional pain. I know I do.

Having pity parties and feeling sorry for ourselves is not productive. We become a victim of our problem when we get in the habit of talking about it. It is like being in a grave with both ends knocked out. It is called a rut! We have the opportunity to change our perspective from being a victim to facing the reality of suffering.

When we suffer, we pray to an unseen God. We pray for help, healing, strength, and comfort. How can a bodiless God stand before us, hold us, put his/her arms around us, and comfort us? Most of us want a person to hold us and soothe the pain. Perhaps we are who Paul means when he referred to Christ being the head of the church, and we being the arms, legs, ears and eyes. We can reach out, touch, hold, hug, and sit with each other. We can produce sound waves with words of comfort and compassion for those who are hurting. We are the body of Christ. So the body does the work that the head tells it to do! This is why twelve step programs like Alcoholics Anonymous, Emotions Anonymous, and others are effective. They are made up of groups of people who have experienced similar suffering who each gain healing from community and sharing.

---

23. Hubbard, American Writer, 1859 to 1915.

Creating steps that move us beyond where we feel stuck allows us to break loose from feeling oppressed by unseen demons. It is being aware of the spirit of Christ and our own experiences of suffering that lead us to acts of understanding, compassion, and simply being with each other.

I by no means have arrived, whatever that means. I am more content to listen and be with another in their pain. I guess if you live long enough, you learn that you can't outrun suffering!

If I have to suffer when I die, I want a room full of people to hold me, hug me, and love me.

Oh, to be Heard

We want to be heard! We want to express our inner thoughts and feelings with our partners. We are attracted to a life partner that we believe is like us, someone who will accept and understand who we are. Most of us soon find out that we are opposites. Often one person is the emotional, expressive one and the other is stoic and practical.

We may be unconsciously looking for a person to create balance in our lives and fill in what we lack. However, the very thing we seek in the other person is what drives us bonkers. The person who is more expressive may say, "Why don't you ever tell me how you feel?" The partner might reply "You need to chill out" or "You get too worked up".

Peace and contentment come back into a relationship when two things happen. First, we need to know who *we* are and strive to be honest about our feelings. Second, we need to be able to accept the other person as they are. If we know and are satisfied with ourselves, we don't really need others to change. We will have more tolerance for who they are. We want to change people when we feel insecure. We think changing them will make us feel better and safer. Wrong! If it is not one thing, it's going to be something else.

Part of accepting and getting to know each other is to be able to hear the other person. To really hear, we need to set aside time without the newspaper, book, television, cell phone or any other interference. Look the other person in the eye and listen.

It seems that when we attempt this, the other person will say something that we feel isn't true or needs further explanation. Often we jump in while they're speaking. We aren't listening. We are planning in our minds our defense. To truly listen, we have to bracket, set aside all our thoughts, and try to be an empty vessel.

Musings

I would tell couples I counseled to let the one who starts speaking finish, even if it takes ten, fifteen, or thirty minutes. "But I will forget what I want to say about something if I wait." I respond, "No, you won't. You will remember what is important when the other finishes. Trust that what is important will come to you. If it doesn't, maybe it wasn't that important." Allowing the other to finish what they are saying may clear up the thing you wanted to comment on. Often if we summarize what we thought we heard when they are finished, they feel validated. If we didn't understand fully, let them clarify. Then we can have our turn while they listen.

It takes faith, love, and acceptance both for you and the other to communicate this way. It is a process of real listening.

Humor

Laughter often brings a sense of relief and freedom that all is well. The best kind of laugh comes from down deep and happens when you hear, read, or see something funny. Tears may run down your face and you can't get your breath. If you tell people about it, they usually don't laugh with abandon as you did. That is because it was something coming from your perception that opened the door to your soul.

Medical studies show hearty laughter leads to improved physical and emotional health. Physically, it shakes up the organs and draws more blood to them. It relaxes the muscles (once your abdominal muscles stop hurting). It can bring a sense of well-being.[24]

This may surprise you: laughter is often a way of dealing with pain. Is it God's gift to us in dealing with the stress of life? We gain insight and common sense from the Book of Proverbs. "A cheerful heart is good medicine, but a crushed spirit dries up the bones." (Prov 17:22) People who see little humor in life often look shriveled up, a step away from being "dry bones."

There is a scene in Robert Heinlein's classic, *Strangers in a Strange Land* where the alien that came to earth could not understand laughter. One day he is at a zoo and watches one monkey pop another monkey on the head. He sees the rest of the monkeys go into hysterical laughter. Then he understands that this is how these strange humans deal with pain.

One of the best forms of laughter comes when we can laugh at ourselves. Just when we think we have succeeded in looking cool and sophisticated, we trip over our own feet. Or go to the toilet in the night, and sit

24. Mayoclinic.org, *Healthy Living*.

in the water because the seat was up. (That one will wake you up! This experience will certainly create more respect from men for the women in the household!)

Wouldn't it be great to have a stand-up comedian preach one Sunday? Here's a bit of humor to lift your day (author unknown):

> An old mountain man and his son visited a mall for the first time. They were amazed by almost everything they saw, but especially the two silver walls that could move apart and back together again. The boy asked his father, "What is this?" The father, never having seen an elevator, responded "Son, I have never seen anything like this in my life, I don't know what it is." While the boy and his father watch wide-eyed, an old lady in a wheel chair rolls up to the moving walls and presses a button. The walls open and the lady rolls between them into a small room. The walls closed, and the boy and his father watch small circles of lights with numbers above the wall light up. They continued to watch the circles light up in the reverse direction. The walls opened again, and a beautiful 24-year-old woman steps out. The father said to his son, "Go get your mother!"

Laugh every day and life will look better, even in hard times.

The Bigger Picture

It is said to be the most printed and sold book in history. That doesn't mean it is the book most read. My dad, a pastor, had a habit. Whenever he picked a book up, he would blow across the top to get the dust off it. He was visiting a parishioner one day, picked up her Bible lying on a table, and without thinking, blew on it. A great cloud of dust drifted down between him and the person. It was an embarrassing moment for both.

My question is, "How do we use the Bible?" Some use it as a bull whip to control the masses with guilt and shame. We have heard the term "proof texting," taking specific verses out of context to prove "God's will." One that comes to mind is, "Do not withhold discipline from a child; if you punish them with a rod, they will not die. Punish them with a rod, and save them from death." (Prov 23:13–14) This one has been used to oppress and abuse children. Pretty scary, isn't it?

If we don't read the Bible with an element of critical thinking, we will likely rely on those we see as authorities for interpretation. There are many instances of that proving dangerous, even fatal (Jim Jones, Heaven's Gate).

Certain stories from the Bible continue to be enlightening in how I choose to live. I believe spiritual influences led to the selection of the sixty-six books of the Bible. Do we also get the bigger picture, the core message or are we stuck in a literal interpretation of specific texts? After reading the Bible, how would you summarize what it is saying?

It tells me to live a life filled with love, healing, compassion, unity, acceptance, grace, and many more positive and creative terms. The Bible can train us in positive and loving living. The key is to be so familiar with its journey from Old Testament shame (Adam and Eve) and jealousy (Cain and Able) to New Testament love (woman at the well, the leper) that we move more easily into a life of love.

After reading it, maybe we can step back and see the forest, rather than using individual trees or branches to beat people over the head.

Savoring Life

Often I don't have enough time to get done all that I think I have to do (or want to do). Since I have Attention Deficit Hyperactive Disorder, my mind is always working. It is an idea mill, one the body can't keep up with. This constant drive is accentuated by living in a society that rewards productivity.

I think there may be a paradox here. If I stop and spend time being in the moment, life will be full enough.

Stop and look deeply at a tree or flower. Absorb it with your whole being in the quietness of the moment. Close your eyes and breathe slowly and deeply. You may notice the air is full of scents that you aren't normally aware of. Savor the flavors and textures of your food as you eat. (We will eat less because the message of a full stomach will have time to get to our brain before we eat too much!) Being in the moment can help soothe the tormented soul as well as open up new life experiences.

I highly recommend a classic book written by Annie Dillard, *Pilgrim at Tinker Creek*. This beautiful book drinks in the world. It won a Pulitzer prize in 1974. It is even more appropriate today for those of us who feel we have to cram every moment with doing. The amount of new information is growing exponentially every year. We may be missing the peace and beauty of what our five senses can provide.

Measuring Up

Out of the hundreds of magazines available, *People* magazine is one of the top ten magazines sold in this country. We are fascinated by celebrities. If given a chance, we clamor to have our picture taken with them, touch their hands as they walk by, or get their autograph. I remember growing up watching girls scream and cry at Elvis's concerts. One of my classmates lost her shoes running beside the train when he was in Knoxville. We called him "The King."

It is interesting that the magazine is called *People* but our response to the celebrities is as if they are something other than human. If we are honest with ourselves, we make them heroes and fall into hero worship.

Why is it that we are drawn to the rich and famous? Is it that they seem to have a life of luxury and glamour? Do we think, "What more could one ask for?" And don't we think, "Wow, I wish I could be in their shoes!"

I have to admit that I have had my own fascination with the famous. No, I don't subscribe to *People* magazine. I am curious about them as common souls like the rest of us. I know that they are just ordinary people. However, we rarely see them in their ordinary day to day lives like the rest of us.

This desire to compare our lives to those of other people isn't limited to just the famous. We are tempted to do it when someone has it better than we do or has something we don't have.

What are we saying about ourselves? If we desire so strongly to be someone else or at least be in their place in life, are we missing who we are and what we have to offer? Jesus said, "You are the salt of the earth. But if the salt loses its saltiness, how can it be made salty again?" (Matt 5:13)

You have your own salt. Shake it.

Repetition

If I write about the same topics or repeat myself, blame it on the Muse. When I read or hear someone talking about how to better experience life or take better care of myself, I say, "Oh that is interesting. I need to do that. I need to change that about my life." And then, it's not long before I forget about it and fall back to most of the old routine. I let the stimulus of life dictate how I respond. I react without thinking. You could say I become unconscious again. Sometimes we have to hear the same thing over and over, and practice it until we experience a shift in the way we live. (I wonder if practice and repetition will ever help me learn things like balancing a checkbook?)

The beauty of writing about the same or similar topics is that it can be helpful to hear something with different examples or from a different perspective. Repetition and changing approaches helps us see things that we might have missed the first time around. This is why some of us enjoy watching the same movie, read the same book, or go back to a place we have been before. Each time we see or learn something different. We can go back to the same spot in four different seasons and see a different beauty each time. One translation of the Bible is called *The Living Bible*. It is a book that feels alive because it keeps on giving and teaching.

Maybe the Muse has its seasons so we can learn lessons to help us through the maze of life. (It helps me to think that I don't have short term memory loss!!)

That Which We Cannot Know

The Creator of the universe and of life cannot be named. Naming something is an attempt to describe or put something within a framework. Often this limits and makes it into an object. The Jews refused to say a name for this Source of life. We have tried to name it, and fallen short. When we put boundaries around the Source of life, we think we have a grasp of it but do we really? When we are humble enough to say we don't know, we have a better chance to experience a connection with this Source of creation. The best I have done in gaining some understanding of this Architect of creation is through my relationships, through the love, acceptance, and compassion I create and receive from others.

You may notice that I haven't used the word "God." It has become too confining because of the limitations we have placed on an image. The word brings up my childhood vision of a man sitting on a golden throne in a long white robe, with a long white beard and a journal, keeping a record of my behavior. (He's probably got carpal tunnel by now.) I know that I am not the only one who has these images.

We even attempt to know each other through labels. You can describe me saying that I am a dad, a psychotherapist, a retired person, or that you see me as compassionate or gregarious. But you still don't know me. We spend a lifetime getting to know those close to us, and yet, don't know them completely.

A man is hiking in the mountains; he has a bushy beard and dirty clothes, and is carrying a three-foot machete. He breaks through the bush into a clearing where there is a cabin. A young woman is on the porch. She turns at the noise, screams, and faints. He carries her to her couch and revives her. Again she screams, thinking he is a vagrant. He is actually a young doctor on a hiking vacation. Soon they begin a relationship (after he shaves and cleans up), but he doesn't tell her he is a physician. She thinks he is without a job at the moment. He finally tells her he wanted her to know him for who he is rather than as a physician because all of the assumptions that go along with that title. (*Moonlight Road* in the *Virgin River Series* by Robyn Carr)

Paul says, "Now we see through a glass darkly, but then face to face...." (1 Cor 13:12) Occasionally we have experiences of "awe" that stop us in our tracks... moments that no words can describe. We also have moments when we learn something surprising about someone we thought we knew. When we are awed by something, we can't find words to describe it. We become more familiar with our "Source of life" over time, especially when we take time to see others beyond their labels.

It takes work to get out of old habits. Look, listen, focus on and be with a person. Maybe you will get closer to "the Source of all that is."

The Beauty of the Journey

We are too hard on ourselves. Those of us who are trying to be better persons sometimes look to be flawless. It ain't going to happen. Jesus said the church is for sinners. The literal Greek interpretation is "missing the mark" [of what God approves][25]. That pretty much includes all of us at some point, wouldn't you say?

The key is to focus on the journey, not having our sights set on arriving (whatever that means). My definition of perfection is "being able to accept where we are in the moment." Enjoy the ride. Focus on what can be learned as we go. If we only look at or worry about the end, we miss many beautiful experiences along the way. If we dwell only on the past, we are stuck and don't move forward.

---

25. Bible Hub, sin.

Musings

I walk my dog almost every day. It is pretty much the same route. There are days that I just want her to walk and not stop as much. Yet, she is teaching me a lesson. She sniffs, looks up into the trees, and has a habit of stopping every six or eight feet to look behind her and see if she missed anything. Each time it seems new to her. She is definitely paying attention to the detail of her surroundings. What a great example of simply being in the moment!

There is a lesson to be learned here about the journey. No matter how many times you take the same trail, there will always be something new to see.

With our heads down and arms pumping, we are only going to see the tops of our shoes, and that scene will only be different if we change shoes!

Perspective

Newspapers and news programs are often built on tragedy and negative events. Take a survey of the headlines for 2014. Most fall in the negative column. This is what sells. This is what the public seems to want.

We are in our car and there is an accident on the side of the road. Traffic slows down; we strain to see what has happened--most assuredly a negative and tragic event.

Many television programs, movies, and video games are based on blowing things up, wrecking automobiles, and figuratively or literally stabbing people in the back. We sit on the edge of our seats in anticipation.

Sadly the producers of *American Idol* believe that exposing people with personality disorders is entertainment. Often individuals are exploited who have Narcissistic Personality Disorder[26]. They have little insight into their level of talent, and may go into a rage when they are not chosen. *Survivor* is a breeding ground for pathological lying and self-serving greed. *The Bachelor* and *The Bachelorette* create fantasies that turn people into objects of desire. Maybe these "reality" programs show us what has become a new reality. Has our perspective of reality been changed by programs that foster isolation rather than unity and love?

I am guilty to some extent of enjoying escapism and romantic wishful thinking. I occasionally read thrillers or watch an action film. However, in our household we have begun to be more selective in what we watch and read.

---

26. Personality disorders, *DSM IV.* 629, 658.

I wonder if we don't lean toward worst-case scenarios so we can feel more in control. We don't like the feeling of being shattered or stunned when we haven't seen disappointment and tragedy coming. Doesn't filling our minds with this kind of stimulus drag us down, rather than motivate us through hope and a more positive outlook? Faith is trust in what has best been called the "nine fruits of the Holy Spirit": Love, Joy, Peace, Patience, Kindness, Goodness, Faithfulness, Gentleness, and Self-Control. (Gal 5:22–23)

I have to work at taking inventory of what I allow into my soul.

Word Power

It seems that a lot of the words used to describe life are more negative than positive. We often describe events with an underlying doubt rather than a sense of hope. Someone might say "We have a picnic planned for tomorrow, but it will probably rain."

Minor changes in our language can make all the difference in experiencing life as a gift, rather as a trial of despair and disappointment. We are in the habit of using the conjunction "but" to connect two parts of a sentence together. "He wrote a great article, but he could have said it in fewer words." Using "but," in most cases, cancels the positive compliment in the first part of the sentence, and focuses on the criticism in the second part. If "and" were used instead, both would be true and equally important. "He wrote a great article *and* he could have said it in fewer words."

Another word that is often used is "problem." "Understanding what she is saying here is a problem." The word "problem" suggests a barrier, and the possibility of struggle in order to solve the difficulty and get beyond it. Would "challenge" be a better word, suggesting a more positive outlook? It affirms that we have the ability to put our talents and tenacity to the test.

I hope your challenges (not *problems*) this week are not overwhelming, and (not *"but"*) they could test your tenacity.

But I Have To!

We ask a lot of ourselves. We are asked to deal with stimuli thrown at us every minute. Our days are filled with activity. I have to do this. I have to go there. I have to see so and so. I have to pick up whatever. It is pretty tiring to be driven by a constant barrage of have to, have to, have to . . . .

Musings

Some of us, out of need and fear, immediately jump into action when someone wants something from us. The fear comes from a deep terror that we will not be loved. Rejection by someone, especially by those we are most connected with, brings with it thoughts of being all alone. It can feel like we are working on the space station, and someone cuts our tether so we are about to be swallowed up in the darkness of space.

Others of us drive ourselves relentlessly to prove we are good or worthy. Our society places a premium on productivity and efficiency. Unfortunately, the bar for productivity is like a carrot on a stick. If we don't feel content with who we are, the goal line of success keeps moving.

I heard a story about a man in a fitness center. He was on the rowing machine. It was digital, so there was a screen showing two boats in a race. One represented his boat and the other the machine's boat. The machine's boat was calibrated to stay just ahead of the man's boat no matter how fast he rowed. He was so driven to win, to succeed, that he kept rowing, faster and faster, so desperate to pass the other boat that the strain caused a heart attack and he died.

My wife has a beautiful question each evening. She asks, "Have you been gentle with yourself today?" Kind of fits with what Jesus said about loving yourself. . . .

Totally Free!

What would you do or how would feel if you won a contest where you could go to any merchant and pick out whatever you wanted free of charge, no strings attached? There used to be contests where someone would win a five, ten, or fifteen minute grocery store shopping spree. They could put as many items into shopping carts as the time would allow, a manic race to "grab stuff." Sounds similar to everyday life!

There are things we need in order to survive. What about those things that we want but don't really need?

We have access to a free gift. It defies logic. It permeates every living thing in existence. It comes from the core of all life, and helps make sense of the journey. Because it defies logic, we have difficulty getting our brain around it. Richard Rohr in his book, *Things Hidden*, calls it "Divine Unmerited Generosity." We have heard it called "grace".

Jesus was born during a time when people thought God's approval was earned by sacrificing animals, paying the temple priests, and performing all kinds of absurd rituals. No wonder he was a threat to the powers of that time when he offered people an unlimited source of free fish and bread, water that would cause you never to thirst, and unconditional love to all, no exclusions, no strings attached.

We don't need to win a contest in order to cram food into grocery carts in a short block of time. We have free food, both literally and figuratively. We gather and have fellowship meals. (I have often felt like a stuffed grocery cart after a church supper!) Celebrating the Lord's Supper is the food and drink that will satisfy our hunger and thirst for security, for wholeness and for a loving family. We often try to fill these needs with things that only leave us empty. If we can truly receive these free gifts, maybe we will find more contentment with what we have.

Some of my happiest times were on my grandmother's farm during the holidays. There would be a gathering of aunts, uncles, cousins, parents, and grandparents sharing a feast. It was a celebration of life in communion. Stories were told. Laughter was contagious. Cousins would play in the front yard. I learned about "divine unmerited generosity" on the farm and at church meals.

I must continually take my life inventory to remember where I am truly fed and loved.

Personal Review

I like the Asian philosophy of the "yin-yang" ☯. The western world often sees the two sides of this circle as polar opposites. In the natural world, they are interdependent and interconnected. Life is full of dualities, male-female, dark-light, up-down, life-death, etc.

We have contrasting thoughts and actions within us: good and bad as well as creative and destructive. I have often wondered why a Creator would want beings with bad qualities? Wouldn't happy, loving, creative, and content creatures be easier? Perhaps having unconditional acceptance of both challenges us to develop, to learn, and to know true love.

If we resist the negative side of ourselves, it only grows like a cancer behind the façade of our pretension. Looking at ourselves gives us a chance to find ways to act and think differently the next time something similar comes up. Just having one side, a circle rolls nowhere.

At the end of the day, consider these: "What could I have done differently today? What would I change? How would I do something differently the next opportunity I have? What do I need to clean up with another person?"

The "yang" side is equally important. Too often we live in the "yin" side, the dark or negative. This is an especially good time to ask these questions: "What did I contribute to life today? What do I feel good about? Where did I share love?"

Beginning this review with the "yin" (the things we want to change), and ending with the "yang" (the things we feel good about), we can thank the Spirit of Goodness. It will likely lead to a better night's sleep, and new challenges for tomorrow.

We are a work in process; and, as some would say, "We are a piece of work".

Simpler Choices

Our choices determine the direction and our quality of life. It is important to stop and think through the next move. Playing the game of chess is a good teacher for looking at the consequences of the next move. A good chess player has to think ahead four or five moves, the top players even more. Living wisely takes real focus and concentration.

Some choices will cause us to have few moves left, such as taking a risky action that causes physical harm or time in prison. As in chess, we are in "check." When we have no moves left, we are in "checkmate" or death.

The choices in life are colorful and exciting because there are so many options. Yet, how often do we take time to look ahead at the possible outcome of our choices? We have so many interesting and exciting options. We may want to experience as many as we can before our body says, "No, you really don't want to do that anymore." Maybe anticipating our mortality drives us to cram as many experiences into life as we can. At some point we have to say we can't do it all and learn to be at peace with what we love to do or are good at.

I have several friends who choose not to own television sets. I suspect they take time to drink in the beauty around them, focus more on their creative interests, and have more time to appreciate people at a deeper level. We don't necessarily have to give up TV entertainment, but we can be more selective about how much time we use it.

The world of marketing feeds off our impulsivity. Spontaneous purchasing puts a smile on the faces of merchants. Yet, how much of our impulse buying soon ends up collecting dust in the garage or donated to a thrift store? I often think there is a wicked purpose in putting the toys and candy right as we enter the cash register lane. It trains us at a very young age to want immediately. It also challenges the patience of parents!

The real challenge for me, after a lifetime of acting first and thinking later, is learning to think first and act with wisdom.

Taking the Blinders Off

There are some who have given most of their energy and their lives to one activity, skill, or interest. For some, that activity, skill, or interest gives them happiness, feeds their being, and rewards them with a sense of accomplishment. For those who are at the very top, there is also fame and fortune.

What happens to those people when they are no longer breaking records, or at their physical and mental peaks? Some sit in despair, asking "What am I going to do now?"

Even if we haven't become the best at our work or craft, most of us will come to a point when we are at a loss as to what's next. Often we don't make time during a busy career to think about other options. It is certainly more difficult to switch gears for those who have lost their jobs and are still in their productive years.

It is the stage most of us go through when we retire. Many people long for the day when they can say what Johnny Paycheck said in his song, "Take This Job and Shove It." A few months or even weeks after they retire, many feel desperate to find something to do.

When I spent time on my grandmother's farm, my uncle would plow the fields with two big Morgan horses. They had leather flaps on the harnesses beside their eyes so they would look straight ahead and plow straight rows. All they could see was in front of them.

The definition of retirement is "to withdraw into privacy or seclusion."[27] We need time to switch our focus and contemplate new options for applying ourselves. Retirement allows time for contemplation, taking the blinders off and, maybe for the first time, seeing three hundred and sixty degrees.

A wide variety of activities are out there as well as an incredible number of resources for learning new skills. There is a school devoted to teaching new skills in Brasstown, North Carolina, called The John C. Campbell Folk School. You can learn everything from woodworking to writing,

---

27. Dictionary.com, "retirement."

basket making to blacksmithing, and storytelling to soap making. It is really a camp for big kids!

Taking on something new outside our comfort zone is to throw our worries to the wind. Jump in with both feet, and be surprised at what you can accomplish!

Or you could be a greeter at Wal-Mart. I love the welcome and help finding what I need.

Street People

>They come, they go,
>Encased in a personal fog,
>Driven by the search to belong,
>Yet afraid to look, to speak, to touch,
>Building houses on sand,
>Lost in the desert of wandering,
>
>A colorful array of life's mix,
>Never sharing in the celebration,
>Passing like shadows in the night,
>They sound so Babylonian,
>Echoing words of desperation,
>
>Cautious attempts to care,
>Twisted voices, tenuous compassion,
>Shouting out warnings of impending doom,
>Just may be a gift of seeing,
>Most walking in abject blindness,
>
>Fighting the dread of annihilation,
>By the cold wasteland of anonymity,
>Pleading for one look—
>An acknowledgement of being.
>
>Where is that love we profess,
>On Sundays, so readily acknowledged,

Yet easily forgotten,
When confronted with the stench,
Of trash bins, alleys, and gutters?

We hurry by appearing occupied,
Lest we be accosted for change,
Putting up a wall of fear or disgust,
Separating us from our brothers and sisters,
Possibly missing an angel's message.

—Edward L. Boye, 2004

The Loudness of Silence

We are not often exposed to silence in our culture. Silence doesn't fit in with the focus our culture places on productivity. It isn't valued where so much emphasis is placed on the individual, on our need to stand out and be heard. Silence is so foreign to us that we become uncomfortable in a group or with another person if more than ten seconds pass without a word. Do your own survey. Mentally count the number of seconds between speech the next time you are in a group or with another person.

There are actually "silence sounds" between the noises. We have to be quiet to hear them, and in the process we develop our "spiritual ears". They speak volumes to our heart.

I have found contemplative prayer meaningful. Contemplative prayer is the inward vision of the soul. Normal verbal activity is curtailed. It relieves us of all effort, and is also known as "centering prayer." To get to one's center is to cease the noise and chaos of the mind. As anyone who practices this will tell you, it takes time and patience. When it happens, there is a soothing flow of peace throughout one's whole being, a feeling of oneness with God. It is a feeling of transcendence.

Does God "get tired" of our chatter or pleading and asking in more traditional prayer? To listen to the silence is to be able to commune with the Spirit of Life, to feel the Presence, and to be at one with God. Being in this place brings peace in times of hurt, pain, despair, fear, and other hardships of life.

Musings

We are told in Rom 8:26, "In the same way, the Spirit helps us in our weakness. We do not know what we ought to pray for, but the Spirit himself intercedes for us with groans that words cannot express."

Have you ever had a time when someone just sat with you, saying nothing, and you felt soothed and embraced just by being in their presence?

Maybe God just wants to sit with us sometimes, and join with us in that "peace that passes understanding." Maybe the answers we seek lie between the words.

Temptation

The dictionary defines temptation as the act of being enticed: "something that causes a strong urge or desire to have or to do something, especially something that is bad, wrong, or unwise."[28] It can be the "monkey wrench" in our effort and desire to be a better person. Is there a being (? the devil) that encourages destructive thoughts and actions? The comedian, Flip Wilson, used to say, "The devil made me do it." If we look at it this way, we are relieved of responsibility for our choices. It is easy to blame our behavior on some outside entity over which we have no control.

God has given us the freedom of choice. We are free, independent souls. It is up to us to make decisions that affect our lives. Acting on that freedom is a statement of God's faith in us.

I believe there are forces of good and evil. We are susceptible to evil or making bad choices when we operate on automatic pilot. Freedom requires focus and being acutely aware of the potential consequences of our choices. It takes hands on the steering wheel, foot available for the brake and accelerator.

If we focus on goodness, love, and creativity during our life challenges, we get our batteries charged. This gives us the strength to more easily walk "the straight and narrow."

One of my favorite poems expresses it beautifully: "Two roads diverge in a wood, and I—I took the one less traveled by, And that has made all the difference."[29]

My experience has been that when I commit myself to choosing the path of creativity, goodness, health, and other such options to improve my life, the intensity of temptation increases. Every time I want to lose a few

28. Merriam-Webster, "temptation."
29. Lathem, " Frost," 105.

pounds or eat healthier, a neighbor with loving intentions brings over a decadent dessert or half of the table at church suppers is filled with sugar and chocolate-laden delicacies.

Has anyone seen a creature with a red suit, horns, long forked tail, and a pitchfork carrying a carrot cake?

Do You Know Me?

I frequently say we have become "human doings." Yet, we still use the term "human beings." "In philosophy, essence is the attribute or set of attributes that make an entity or substance what it fundamentally is, and which it has by necessity, and without which it loses its identity."[30] I love God's answer to Moses when he asks, "What name shall I say to the children of Israel?" God says to tell them, "*I am who I am*. This is what you say to the Israelites. *I am* has sent me to you." (Exod 3:12–14)

We define ourselves by our roles. Often the first thing someone asks you is "What do you do?" Is it because we are uncomfortable with the kind of conversation it takes to "know" another person? When we met as ministers in the United Methodist church, the greeting was, "Where are you?" referring to "What church do you serve?" It was about where you were on the ladder of an unspoken caste system. I often gave the facetious reply, "I am right here."

Just relying on labels limits who we are. Labels put us in neat little boxes with titles of plumber, preacher, teacher, produce manager, parent, and politician. Labels on the outside of the box describe what is in it. However, labels are only a brief description. You have to open the box to see what it looks like, how it feels, how it works, and what its nuances are. This takes time.

I like the show on television, *The Voice: The Blind Auditions*. The judges sit with their backs to the singers so they won't be influenced by their looks. They listen intently to their singing. They want to hear the soul of the person's voice, the essence of their talent.

What is one's essence? What is the "I am?" Spend time with a person to know their "I am". Get the essence of a person by listening without the interference of a busy mind calculating what we want to say next. In time we learn the person's habits, feelings, and responses to situations. We walk

---

30. Wikipedia, "essence."

with them through tragedy and triumph. Bonding takes place when souls shake hands.

Soul mates aren't just exclusive to romantic relationships. Take an opportunity to walk this journey with soul brothers and sisters. I had the greatest feeling when a buddy signed my birthday card, "To my best friend." We have spent a lot of time together.

The road to one's being is longer than the one to a person's labels. The label game is like skipping rocks across a pond.

I am!

Nothing but Net

It amazes me every time I watch college or NBA basketball that a ball thirty inches in circumference, weighing twenty-two ounces, and a little over nine and a third inches in diameter, can go straight through a hoop that is eighteen inches in diameter, even when the ball is thrown from twenty-four feet (the three point line). That leaves four and one third inches leeway on any side of the basketball if it goes through the hoop dead center. The basketball lingo for that is, "nothing but net". It is the perfect shot. Of course, any old way to get that ball through the hoop helps win the game.

What about the game of life? Sometimes it feels just like that, a game. We have to jump through many hoops in a lifetime. At times it feels like we bounce around the rim holding our breath, hoping we will drop through. At other times we are slammed against the backboard and, if we are lucky, drop through the hoop; otherwise, we bounce off, and have to try again. Occasionally, when we experience a "nothing but net" moment, we are given inspiration to continue, wanting to be a part of the excitement of living.

There are times in playing the game of life that we find ourselves with hands on our knees, dripping sweat, and sucking air. This is likely the time to go to the bench to rest and gather our thoughts. Most of us are so set on winning that we continue to run up and down the court in a frenzy. We get sloppy, missing more shots, becoming more prone to injury and burn-out. Smart players go to the bench for a while, talk to the coach, and get support before getting back into the game.

Playing the game of life not only involves excitement and disappointment, but the need to go to the bench to gather our thoughts, rest our bodies, and listen to what the Coach has to say about how we are playing.

The Coach would likely say, "Lie down in green pastures, sit beside still waters, and your soul will be restored." (Ps 23:2)

We pump our fists, jump around, and shout when we do succeed in getting "nothing but net." From time to time, be wise enough to go to the bench, catch your breath, drink some water, and listen to the Coach.

Yeah!

Epidemic Rage

"Going postal" is a term coined in the past few decades. It is a tragic term, referring to someone going into a workplace, school, or mall and shooting people.

When I look at television, movies, even some books, and especially video games that base their appeal on violence, it takes little imagination to see how violence has increased in our society.

I am stunned by some of the video games, their main audience being children, teens, and young adults. The person playing is rewarded with points and access to a higher level of skill, based on how many beings they can blow up or splatter. The rapid increase in technology has led to increasing vividness of the portrayed reality.

If we are consistently subjected to violence long enough, we become desensitized to it. A person's compassion and moral structure will be eroded. When the line between game and reality gets crossed, tragedy is often the result.

What do we blame—the person creating or playing the game, the parents, or a person's living situation? Maybe we should look no further than our choices of what we support with blind eyes and numb minds because we think these incidents are so far removed from us.

Movie ratings clearly tell us their content. In recent years, there is a warning at the end of advertisements for some television shows: "*Viewer discretion advised. This show may contain some scenes that some viewers may find disturbing.*" What more wake-up call do we need? If no one watches, the show will be cancelled. The best censor comes from within.

We see news coverage of a school shooting. We shake our heads and say, "What is this world coming to?" If we take time to take it in, we hurt for those involved. We even pray for their peace and comfort through their shock and grief. However, reality knocks us to the ground when it is someone we know. It stops our world in that moment.

Even if we don't know anyone involved, I hope we will stop, think and pray, asking what we can change about our lives to diminish rage that "goes postal." What does God require of us? "My sacrifice, oh God is a broken spirit; a broken and contrite heart that You will not despise."(Ps 51)

Self-Importance

I have often marched to the beat of the drum of unconventional thinking. I have been proud of being different, in challenging the "shoulds" of life. Pretension doesn't win me any friends. It is the fancy cloak that covers the nakedness of truth.

Lest we be victims of our own self-righteousness, we need to look in the mirror at our actions and protestations. Jesus said volumes on this subject: "You hypocrite, first take the plank out of your own eye, and then you will see clearly to remove the speck from your brother's eye." (Matt 7:5) He didn't care much for the pompous pretensions of the Pharisees.

There are similar sayings: "That which we dislike in others may be what we dislike about ourselves." We quote Shakespeare's "The lady doth protest too much, me thinks"[31] to mean that people suspect something *is* true when someone strongly insists that it is not. I often take a closer look at my motivation if I catch myself trying to shock or impress others.

When we are able to accept the truth about ourselves, the good as well as the bad, we will be less critical of others, and have less need to stand out. If we are ok with ourselves, we don't want others to be anyone but who they are. Our need to change other people is usually based on a lack of self confidence. Being comfortable with who we are opens up a freedom to receive others. We become more willing to hear their truth. They no longer need to defend themselves against our criticism as they sense more freedom to share who they are.

Shocking people with outrageous behavior sets us up to be cut off from others. Boasting about meeting someone famous, or worse, having a wall full of pictures made with celebrities can demonstrate how unimportant we feel. We are still a shadow beside an idol. And we know what Jesus said about idol worship!

I have dropped a name or two thinking that it would make me look good. The absurdity of that is dawning on me. The fascination with fame

---

31. Shakespeare, *Hamlet*.

and fortune comes too close to worshiping false gods. Doing so takes away from the beauty and uniqueness of who we are.

Hey, did I tell you that I have a friend whose neighbor's uncle's son met the Pope! And your point is?

Enchantment

Most of us live our lives chasing what we call success. Unfortunately, we have a very narrow definition of success in our culture. One is seen as successful for things like making the news, reaching the Olympics, or being labeled as an authority.

Success is relative. We all have had success: learning to read, repairing something, bringing out happiness in someone else, or simply accomplishing our daily "do list." Success to someone in Somalia is finding water or the next meal.

Yet the above successes, you say, are just part of living. Most of us don't find them very exciting, often classifying them as the mundane. They don't get us into *People* magazine.

I would like to introduce another word, perhaps more meaningful than success. That word is "enchantment." We have lost the experience of being enchanted. The dictionary describes enchantment as "a feeling of great delight or a feeling of being captivated, or under a spell."[32] Many of us have only allowed ourselves to feel enchantment in fairy tales.

How often have you felt the magic of sweeping the floor, washing a dish, tying a shoe, forming letters on a piece of paper, or doing any other simple act of life? For most of us it's been rarely, I expect as our minds are somewhere else. Can we shut out thoughts, sounds, and other distractions so we can focus our attention to the simple task at hand?

Watching the soap bubbles in a sink of dish water with a rainbow of colors, or seeing scattered dust, dirt, and debris formed into a mound, or watching our hands form the loops needed to tie our shoes can be magic. Remember the pride and glee you had when you first learned to tie your shoes as a child? That child in you may have been covered over by the expectations of a society that puts more value on being serious and mature.

Jesus said that one has to be childlike to enter the kingdom of heaven. (Matt 18:3) Maybe he is telling us we can be enchanted with the gift of his Father's creation. The kingdom of heaven is right before us.

32. *Your Dictionary*, "enchantment."

Musings

Life can be magic. It can captivate us and fill us with delight if we allow ourselves to see it happening right before our eyes.

Think I will go read a book by someone who describes the enchantment of life, a sorcerer of scenes of simple delight. Robert Frost is one such wizard.

Sacred Ground: Part I

Most of us try to create a comfortable life. A lot of us strive to be the best, to be at the top of our skill and talent. Many have had dreams at one time or another of being recognized for excellence. One has only to look at the auditions for *American Idol* to see thousands who dream of greatness as we so narrowly define it in this society. Those who have tokens of having reached their goals (certificates, trophies and even t-shirts) display them for all to see.

Those who reach the "top" will eventually lose to someone better, someone younger, or by some limit thrown at us by our body. There is nothing wrong with doing the best we can, being the best we can be. The problem comes when we formulate an identity being on a pedestal. "Living" up there for much of our life increases the chance of crashing to the ground where most of us reside.

Some can be at the top and survive the attention and pressure. They know that being there constantly is a hazard to a real life. They find ways to balance reality with fantasy. They create ways of staying grounded in something greater than ego fodder.

My wife and I watched a movie that very beautifully speaks to the challenges of staying grounded in something greater than our accomplishments. I highly recommend the movie, *Seven Days in Utopia*, starring Robert Duvall. The movie is an adaptation of the book *Golf's Sacred Journey* by David L. Cook.

The movie portrays the theme of our striving to reach the best in us. The main message is learning how to reach the best in us, feel it and trust it, as opposed to thinking it to death. If you play music and only think about your playing, you end up being a good or even great technician. When one senses the mood of a song, feels the music, and trusts one's ability to let those feelings flow from the soul, one has reached spiritual expression. This is true not just in music, but in art, sports, writing, or any endeavor where you are creatively using your talent or skill.

We are not made to live completely in a world of sensing, feeling and trusting, but we can go there from time to time. For me, those times have felt like I was walking on sacred ground. Words cannot express the experience, but if you have been there, you know.

Sacred Ground: Part II

Today I continue musing about *Sacred Ground*. David L. Cook, author of *Golf's Sacred Journey*, reads a quote from his book on a video. It was so moving and profound that I feel the need to share it. He says,

> "I was being anointed by a world obsessed with putting people on a pedestal. And when a man receives it, unbeknownst to him, he accepts the public exposition that comes from the inevitable great fall. We live and perform on a stage before a sick, voyeuristic media of hidden faces, hiding in the shadows of each tragic demise . . . No man was made for a pedestal. That spot had been reserved before the beginning of time for One. No man can carry the weight of glory, nor is he supposed to. All champions fall when talent fails to hold up under the pressure or when age or death eventually prevails in this mortal state. And when it happens, early or late, another is anointed and the cycle proceeds." [33]

Why is it that we are so fascinated by the lives of entertainers and sports figures? We are especially drawn to stories of when they "fall from grace." We line up like automobiles in traffic slowly passing a wreck. Maybe we want to know that such figures are vulnerable beings like ourselves. Maybe we want to be reminded that we all have our limits and are mortal. All life is a cycle of living and dying, and we are part of it.

The challenge is to get to the place where we see that our bodies are "space suits" that help us work on this "space station" made of rock and dirt. What is inside the "suit" is the essence of your being, protected for the journey of eternity.

You can go to the website (www.didhemaketheputt.com), and hear Cook read more very moving words of spirit from his book. However, I suggest you read the book or see the movie before watching the website video. Doing so will make the reading more powerful.

The movie can be streamed or ordered from Netflix. It makes a statement about how to live a beautiful, more meaningful life. It is one of those

33. Cook, *Utopia*.

rare films that move us beyond the ordinary to the profound. I sat for a while after finishing the movie, feeling like I had been given a peek beyond the curtain of this world, a glimpse of the sacred.

Take care of your "space suit." It protects something beautiful!

False Gods

How do we spend our time and energy? What do we get caught up in? What feeds our desires? Where is our passion? What do we feel is important enough to put time into? What do we worship? All of these define our world view.

We continue to develop language that expresses what we worship. We see them every day—*sale, clearance, below cost, lowest prices, black Friday*, etc. These words appear on television and in the news much more often than *praise, joy, comfort, compassion, faith, communion*, etc. I am certainly not an old-fashioned religious zealot—far from it; however, the contrast in our use of these two different sets of words speaks to how we spend our energy and often, what our souls pursue.

We have carried the innate "programming" of being "hunters and gatherers" to new heights of absurdity. I am no stranger to the seduction of getting a "deal." Maybe the notion of getting a deal, saving money or finding the lowest price is driven by the fear that we won't have enough to survive. Maybe we like the feeling of power when we believe we are besting the seller: "Boy, did I take him to the cleaners!" It seems like an oxymoron to say I have saved money when I just reduced my cash flow by however much I paid for the item "on sale!" I am not sure who "cleaned" whom.

My first experience in stalking a deal was when I was about twelve years old. Our local department store advertised a "door buster" sale for winter coats at five dollars each. I needed a new coat for school. I was at the store early enough to be first in line–about thirty minutes before opening. A number of people lined up behind me, mostly adults. I saw the man coming with his keys to open the door. He looked a little tense. He put the key in the lock, turned it, pulled the door quickly back while dashing out of the way. I was forcefully pushed aside as I watched the large man behind me literally fly parallel onto the table with his arms open like a huge mechanical scoop taking more than half the coats with him. Suddenly, the man was transformed before my eyes into a long-haired creature, with mastodon teeth around his neck, holding a bunch of animal skins, and shaking his spear in victory.

"Their land is filled with idols; they bow down to the work of their hands, to what their own fingers have made." (Isa 2:8)

Sitting in the Ashes

We feel helpless when someone is hurting or has a loss. Our society conditions us to want to help or express some comforting words. We also don't want others to hurt because of our own experience: we know how painful it is. So feelings of awkwardness come up when we are in the presence of someone experiencing the kind of pain that comes from the depths of their being.

The story of Job represents just about every loss and hurt one can experience in life. Talk about someone who has gone through a *mess of hurtin'*. He was sitting in the ashes of the remains of his life. His friends came to sit with him: "Then they sat on the ground with him for seven days and seven nights. No one said a word to him, because they saw how great his suffering was." (Job 2:13) There is power in being able just to sit with someone in their ashes, a power that we don't understand well.

My father was in the hospital, having gone through major abdominal surgery. He looked like he was sewn back together with baling wire. He was obviously in a lot of pain. In my naïve attempt to have compassion, I said, "I know how you feel." He replied, "The hell you do!"(This was my minister father who rarely used such expressive terms. So I knew he was really hurting.) My words were a common response to someone in pain, but also false. I knew he was in pain, but truly didn't know or personally feel his physical pain. So I just sat with him. Not having him be alone in those desolate ashes of pain probably did more to lessen or distract him from its intensity than any words I could have said.

Sitting with someone in their emotional pain is to say, "I want to be with you in your hurting." Your silence brings you closer to where they sit at this moment in their life. It says you are willing to share in the ashes with them. This experience of being with the person breaks down the barriers we create by wanting to do or say something. Words become so much chatter in the world of pain.

Musings

> Let's learn to go against our natural tendency to "fix things" and learn to face our own uncomfortable awkwardness. Let's learn to truly meet those we love by just sitting with them in the ashes of their lives.

The Home

She sits and seems to stare
    At life in awe!
We see her confused
    And making embarrassing mistakes.
She speaks of a tree that appears
    As if it wasn't there before
We humor her, a glance at each other
    With knowing feelings
The tree reminds her of a time
    In her youth with a boy
We feel she has wandered again
    Back to the recesses of a muddled mind
Again she mentions that tree anew
    As if it suddenly grew in the last two minutes
We seem bored
    But resigned to the fractured wanderings
Then she suddenly moves off to tell someone
    They cannot go into the garden, it is hers.
We go to attempt to explain her confused state
    Yet, they seem to respond to her spirit not her words
And a conversation ensues
    As if a new family reunion was taking place
She now is at peace in sharing "her" garden
    We begin to urge her back into her room
It is nap time
    She lingers with the flowers
Touching each one as if some shared communication was taking place
    She suggests that we consider
Buying a nice house across the road
    The breeze and trees are beautiful here

We leave her at the invisible line at the elevator door
> So as to not set off the "warning buzzer."

The look is one of gratitude for a brief respite
> From the strange babblings of her floor mates

And a longing for a lingering moment more of touch and presence.

—Edward L. Boye, 1998

Where is the Field Manual?

When we are traversing life's journey, sometimes we get lost. (These days our first impulse is to Google for an answer to our problem.) At the worst of our pain, we pray agonizingly, "Help me God! Show me some sign." And then, there is silence.

There is no rule book, instruction, or operating manual in how to deal with each situation of life. There is no book that says, "Go to Chapter 23, Section 14, Paragraph 3, and discover what to do next."

Some would say the Bible is a field manual to life. Then they attempt to make the Bible into a narrow set of rules for living life. However, the Bible is open to interpretation. One scripture can be interpreted in as many ways as there are those reading it. Scholars have argued for years over specific texts as they attempt to find the best English words to describe a Greek or Hebrew word that doesn't have an English equivalent.

We all carry wounds received in the battles of learning to navigate through each day. Some wounds from childhood are buried deep. They can pop up unexpectedly to knock us flat on our *"but tocks,"* as Forrest Gump would say. The wound gets opened once again much later.

There are places to gain understanding of these scars we all carry: therapy, reading, self-reflection, groups, etc. Yet, we still have to live with the scars.

The Bible is a great source of basics that can help us heal the wounds. Notice I didn't say "cure." To cure is to get rid of the wound. To heal is to accept and live with the scar tissue over the wound. Healing comes when we apply the basic biblical concepts: forgiveness (of self and others), trust, faith, hope, and love. The most difficult point in our pain is when we don't know what to do, and have arrived at the end of our rope. All that is left is to turn it over to God and have faith that we will get through it.

Musings

However, most of us are so independent that we don't know how to let go. We keep struggling to find an answer, keep beating our heads against the wall, and keep trying to understand. Do you ever get tired of trying? Maybe it is God's way of saying, "Come to me, all you who are weary and burdened, and I will give you rest. Take my yoke upon you and learn from me, for I am gentle and humble in heart, and you will find rest for your souls. For my yoke is easy and my burden is light." (Matt 11: 28–30) Stop trying so hard!

Some things just can't be Googled!

Honoring Your Body

Our bodies are containers for our journeys through life. They are beautiful containers. I have often spoken of the body as our "space suit." An astronaut has to be extremely cautious with his or her suit when working in space. A snag or rip could mean death.

As you already know, our physical bodies are no less vulnerable to damage. Yet, we often take risks without thinking of the consequences. A lot of us never get beyond a developmental phase of adolescence called "personal fable." This is the phase in adolescence where one feels immortal, leading to taking risks without forethought of any consequences.

As adults, we may stop testing how fast we can drive our cars around the next curve without knowing the sharpness of the curve or how far our steering wheels will turn. We may not jump off a bridge into unfamiliar waters without checking the depth first. However, are we really aware of our body's needs or of the times we abuse it? Often we speed down the road race of life, and put concern for our bodies at the bottom of our priorities.

How can we honor one's own or someone else's body. It takes noticing our bodies, feeling their presence, recognizing their transitions, and cherishing the miraculous gift we have, "for I am fearfully and wonderfully made." (Ps 139:14)

A friend of mine told me a beautiful story of honoring the functions of one's body. A father came home one day after work, and his wife told him that their daughter just started her first menstrual flow. He ran upstairs and knocked on his daughter's door. She said, "Come in". He said for her to get dressed, that he was taking her out to dinner. She said, "Why?" He replied, "To celebrate your becoming a woman." What a beautiful gift to honor a passage of life that we still have some pretty archaic feelings about.

Taking good care of our bodies doesn't necessarily mean our lives will be prolonged. Even vegetarians and exercise junkies can have heart attacks or die young. Many of us do take good care of our bodies so we can have a full life while we are on this journey.

Maybe we need to create rituals that honor the body: taking a walk noticing how our muscles move and carry us through the beauty of the earth; soaking in a bubble bath and seeing it as a cleansing of the day's worries and stresses; savoring each bite of food while mind tracing the process it took to get it from the ground or tree to your plate, thanking all those involved in that process.

Do you have a beautiful body? The answer will come when you cherish and honor it!

Freedom from Fear

We are vulnerable. We don't know what is going to happen next. We can plan and anticipate, but we don't know if things will work out to fit our vision. A lot of the time they don't. Woody Allen is quoted as saying, "If you want to make God laugh, tell him about your plans."[34]

We obviously aren't in control of the journey. How often have you heard someone say, "If you told me a year ago that I would be where I am, I would have told you that you were crazy!" Sometimes it is a surprise, and other times, a shock.

We often live in fear because we feel vulnerable. We spend a lot of time looking for ways to feel secure while we attempt to predict the future. I remember the futility of people's stockpiling food and water right before the year 2000. Remember, Y2K?

Forethought and planning are a necessary part of being responsible for ourselves, and for others around us. Yet, if we look at the amount of time we spend worrying about whether we will have enough money to live on, being obsessive about germs for fear of becoming ill, making sure we have enough food, and working at avoiding the "grim reaper," we realize that we rob ourselves of living life with a sense of freedom and joy.

A lot of people who have had near-death experiences will tell you that they now notice things about life that they missed before. They describe colors as being more vivid, the aroma of food as more intense, and have increased awareness of the sounds of life. They live with less fear. It is as if

34. Allen, "plans."

a cloud has been lifted from their senses. They seem to live with a powerful love for all of life in their hearts.

Where do we find comfort in this uncertainty? How do we experience a vibrant life, one with a sense of freedom and joy, with feelings of peace and calm acceptance?

After quoting seven words in another musing from Psalm 139, I reread the whole Psalm. I believe many of the answers to these questions are found in this incredibly beautiful Psalm.

I invite you to read it, and go out and dance with a new sense of abandon!

Retirement?

When you were younger, did you ever look at someone over fifty and think, "That's an old person!" For those of you over fifty, think back to those thoughts. Do you now feel like you are as old as you thought those people looked? I am here now, when I am supposed to be *old* like the images I had as a teen. But I don't feel as old as I thought those people were supposed to think and feel (except for some mornings).

I rarely feel grumpy, dried up, or slow. I don't drive like I am on a farm tractor. My teeth don't sit in a glass of water at night. I have slowed down a little, and I have a few more aches and pains that follow me around. Yet, through these eyes I see a beautiful and vibrant world, one full of adventure and mystery yet to be discovered. I will probably not swim the English Channel or climb Mount Everest, but I still have curiosity, wonder, and fascination about life.

I have had adventures: parasailing, being in a hot air balloon, sliding down a five-story waterslide, and owning a motorcycle. Occasionally I still want to grease a door knob or slip a "whoopee" cushion into someone's chair. (Those things are electronic now. What's this world coming to?)

I have also discovered that the retirement I envisioned in my youth doesn't exist. Most days I wonder why I don't have time to get the things done I had planned. However, retirement has given me control of my multifunction job description.

I am now a chronicler of life as a writer and photographer, an agricultural engineer, a physical trainer, the director of a one-person think tank, one of a group of writers of life's comedy show (we meet once a week), a political analyst, a foreign correspondent, and a household engineer.

Sometimes when I go to work, I just sit around and read. It must be a government job. I still get a check once a month!

I heard once that old people are the richest people in the world, because they have a mouth full of gold, a head full of silver, and a belly full of gas! Whoever said that must know firsthand!

Life is good!

When Love Rules

Often anger seems a reasonable response to certain people and situations. We become incensed when a neighborhood guard shoots a sixteen-year-old kid or a soldier kills innocent men, women, and children. These are truly tragic and heart-rending. On the other hand, how do we feel when someone quickly drives into a parking place we were just approaching, cuts us off in traffic, or threatens us physically or verbally. Often anger is an immediate response to all of these situations. We want revenge.

We feel compassion for a victim without thinking. What about the perpetrator? What if we send love to both parties? A rare few pray for all those involved. If we look deeper, we will see that the persons causing the violence have been wounded at some time in their life. This is not to justify the meanness and tragedy that has happened. It is just a way to recognize that all persons are children of the Creator.

Negativity breeds more negativity. We are beings of energy. Are we aware that our thoughts and feelings send out waves of energy? The energy of love not only touches that place in all of us where love may be buried under abuse and scars, but it can also cancel out negative energy. Love is truly one of God's miracles but we need help in bringing it to bear in all of life.

An experience called the Maharishi Effect[35] takes place when just one per cent of the population of a town focuses on thoughts of harmony, based in thoughts and feelings of love. The "effect" is a decrease in crime, violence, accidents, and illness. Improvement in economic conditions occurs. Extensive studies have proven this with each demonstration.

I observed someone replacing anger with a positive response toward another. Some years ago, I was riding with my business partner. He pulled out from a side street into a double lane road. It looked as if he were going into the second lane. A truck was coming down that lane. The passenger leaned out the window shaking his fist, calling us negative names. My

---

35. Wikipedia, "Transcendental Meditation."

partner responded by saying, "I am so sorry. I didn't mean to upset you." The guy's demeanor changed from rage to a softer countenance. Then he said, "God bless you."

Every time you want to respond to a situation with negative feelings or thoughts, try intentionally replacing that energy with compassion and love. It will likely have a "Maharishi Effect," which we can also call a "Jesus Effect," as that was what his thirty-three life years were all about.

I hope your day is full of warmth, cheerfulness, and many blessings.

Resourcefulness

When we take time to be aware of our surroundings, being aware of each moment—whether driving, sitting in a classroom, or watching someone apply a skill—we are acquiring an encyclopedia of information that can make life easier, more fun, and more interesting.

Most of my life I have probably been a nuisance to home repairmen as they come to fix something that is no longer working. As they work, I watch intently and I ask questions. Like a sponge, I absorb all that is going on. I am curious, fascinated with life, and how things work. I have a better chance next time of fixing things myself.

One story comes to mind. We had a clock repairman come from a short distance to tone down the chime sounds of our beloved grandfather clock. I stood there watching as he opened the door to the clock, looked at the hammers, reached into his bag, and brought out a sheet of green felt dots. He stuck one to each hammer. He tested the chimes and they sounded just right. He handed me the bill for sixty dollars. I guess I looked a bit stunned. He grinned and said, "Fifty cents worth of material, and fifty-nine dollars and fifty cents worth of experience."

Being resourceful, full of initiative, and good at problem-solving, especially in difficult situations, gives us a well-stocked tool bag for life.

We formalize learning by creating schools. Do we stop studying when we graduate? The school of life continues. There are tests. The answers come when we apply what we have learned. Sometimes we don't succeed. (I don't like the word fail. It has bad connotations.)

When we don't succeed, we don't have to go back a grade. We get to try as many times as we like. There are no grades or red marks on a paper. We accumulate knowledge, skill and resourcefulness.

MacGyver was one of my favorite television shows. Made years ago, the show was about a resourceful man who used everyday materials to solve complex problems. He always had duct tape and a Swiss army knife.

We have been given a wealth of materials and an incredible "computer." If we take time to observe, we can be incredibly ingenious.

Make sure you always have duct tape!

A Living Novel

You are a book. You are a novel, something "new and different, often in an interesting, unusual, and inventive way."[36] Each of us is different, interesting, unusual, and inventive. Jesus said, "Indeed, the very hairs of your head are all numbered". (Luke 12:7) (My "inventory" in that area isn't as great as it used to be!) It was just his way of saying how unique we all are.

As a psychotherapist, I loved seeing clients. Hearing about their lives was like reading a new novel. Each person we meet can be an adventure far more fascinating than any television series. If we are as focused on each new person who shares with us as we are on our favorite TV shows, a new fascinating world will open up for us. That is, if we aren't caught up in planning what to say when they take a breath. Notice that people are more willing to share their stories with us as well. We all want to feel significant, to be heard.

The psychologist Erik Erikson named eight stages that we go through in life. The eighth stage speaks to the way our "book" can turn out. It is called the stage of "ego integrity versus despair." When we look back and feel satisfaction with our lives with few regrets, we often have a sense of our integrity as well as feeling complete. If we feel we have wasted our time, and have many regrets, we may be left with bitterness. Don't you feel that most lives have contributed something to the whole, even if the individual doesn't feel they accomplished what was wanted? Even a small turn toward creativity and loving is always a plus.

I like the quote from an unknown author, "One day your life will flash before your eyes. Make sure it's worth watching."

So what is the theme of the "book" you are writing? Will it be a best seller? Will it have a happy ending? Will you be satisfied with the time you spent "writing" it?

---

36. Microsoft Encarta, "novel."

Musings

Those of you who are reading this are probably still alive. Since you are the author of your life (your "novel"), you have time to change your direction to one with a better ending. Good "writing" takes time, concentrated thought, review, and editing (correcting errors). By the way, we all have the same Editor. It is important to stop writing from time to time, and listen to the Editor.

Certainty or Risk?

We put a lot of work into making our lives safe and secure. We make lists, plan, and think ahead about the way we want life to be for us. As we crouch behind the walls of flimsy certainty, we miss opportunities to experience a larger, more exciting world.

A certain amount of planning is a responsible endeavor. However, if we count totally on those plans, we never cease to be surprised (or sometimes shocked) that when we get "there", it is a foreign place. Putting our "eggs in one basket" is to live in naiveté. We usually experience at least disappointment, sometimes despair.

One must have courage to take risks and walk outside one's comfort zone, being curious when things don't work out as we envision. It is an opportunity to learn, to take new paths. Even though we risk having a painful experience, we can learn from it. Certainty can be a dull path with few rewards.

I came across this poem some years ago that speaks about venturing out into the mystery of living.

> **Risk**
>
> "To laugh is to risk appearing a fool,
>
> To weep is to risk appearing sentimental.
>
> To reach out to another is to risk involvement,
>
> To expose feelings is to risk exposing your true self.
>
> To place your ideas and dreams before a crowd is to risk their loss.
>
> To love is to risk not being loved in return,
>
> To live is to risk dying,
>
> To hope is to risk despair,
>
> To try is to risk failure."

But risks must be taken because the greatest hazard in life is to risk nothing.
The person who risks nothing, does nothing, has nothing, is nothing.
He may avoid suffering and sorrow,
But he cannot learn, feel, change, grow or live.
Chained by his servitude he is a slave who has forfeited all freedom.
Only a person who risks is free.
The pessimist complains about the wind;
The optimist expects it to change;
And the realist adjusts the sails."[37]

—William Arthur Ward

Voices

I hear voices in my head. No one else can hear them. They talk to me daily. Sometimes they tell me how stupid I am; others say how clever I am. Unfortunately, they say "you should" and "if only" a lot of the time. When I am with other people, these voices tell me how wrong or ignorant or less than I am, or the reverse. Before you think I am hallucinating or are psychotic, what are you doing right now? You are listening to the voices in your head! I bet they are saying, "This is weird." "Ed has gone over the edge this time." "Yada, yada, yada . . . ."

Who are these voices? They are the voices of the past, voices of those who told us their views of how to be in life, voices of their expectations. Some of these voices were helpful to encourage us to venture out, learn new things, and take some risks.

Sometimes these voices seem to speak all at once. Our heads feel like the verbal chatter on the floor of Congress. These voices are especially loud when someone else is talking. They are in a strategy session telling us what to say next. When this happens we can't hear, know, feel, or sense who the other person is. At these times we want to scream "shut up!"

We will always have these internal guides. Some of them lead us to the "high road" and some the "low road." It is up to us to be in charge instead of allowing them to run our lives. Where do we get the strength to take over and direct these voices of chaos?

---

37. Ward, American Writer, 1921 to 1994.

Musings

I have heard of One who has said He is "a still small voice within". (1 Kgs 19:11–13 KJV) I am feeling better already because of the words "still" and "small." This Voice speaks with compassion, and brings peace and calmness. This Voice says there is a "peace . . . that transcends all understanding". (Phil 4:7) I found this peace as a child on my grandmother's farm on sunny days with white puffy clouds passing over as I lay in the green grass beside still waters.

Be careful! Some voices will try to mimic the Voice of peace to gain control over your actions. You can tell the difference because this Voice speaks of all things positive, loving, and creative.

Visualize yourself going along, slapping duct tape over these wayward voices. Then it becomes so quiet that "a still small voice" can easily be heard.

God's Will?

We are told to follow God's will. How does one determine God's will? How do we know what God wants us to do in a given situation?

The more conservative Christians will say, "Just read the Bible. It is the inerrant word of God." I am cautious about interpreting the Bible literally as I continue to experience how much interpretation is involved. I have heard a variety of interpretations for particular verses of scripture.

The more liberal churches might say, "Just follow what is in your heart." This mantra could lead to more narcissistic or self-serving interpretation.

So who is right? What is the truth? How do we clearly "hear" the wisdom of that Power that lies beyond this "soup" of opinions? Most of us who claim to have a religious faith anchor our attempt to hear and be led by the Bible. We commonly hear the Bible called "the inspired word of God."

However, there are layers to go through in our attempt to know what God is telling us: God's inspiration, man's writing, scholars' translations, ministers' interpretations, and our own attempt to make sense of it after it has been passed through so many filters.

I look at the spirit and repeating themes of this ancient book of wisdom. The outstanding themes we see are forgiveness, empathy, trust, faith, honor, service, and love. These words call for a positive interpretation.

When theological study is put through the grinder of critical thinking, we are left with a lot of questions. We have to learn to live with the questions, and develop faith in the core goodness of spiritual beings as well as in a Higher Power who influences life in mysterious ways.

The New Testament part of the Bible gives us a example of one who demonstrated how forgiveness, empathy, trust, faith, honor, service, and love can be put into action.

The Bible is a good read because each time we read it, new thoughts or understandings pop into our mind, make us smile, and give us comfort in spite of the remaining questions. It can make the confusion of life more bearable.

More Than I Anticipated

We are an industrious lot. We love to take on projects and create things. Do you have grandiose thoughts about getting things done in a projected amount of time? My mind often tricks me into believing I am between eighteen and thirty-five. When I take on a project, the next day my body reminds me that I am no longer in that age range.

Often this malady strikes the *Silent Generation* (births 1925–1945) and the *Baby Boomers* (births 1946–1964), although no one is immune. "*The Silent Generation* is described as being highly ambitious with a need for achievement, power, and status."[38] "*Baby boomers* control over 80% [of this country's] personal financial assets and [account for] more than half of all consumer spending."[39] Both generations are said to be stressed-out as a result of the demands to be successful in a consumer world. They have spent a lifetime filling every minute.

I am learning when I get into a project and run out of steam, I need to walk away. Most of these projects will be there the next time I feel spunky enough to tackle them. I am not always successful in walking away as I see one more thing that could be completed. There are too many "one more things." By that time my "get up and go has done got up and went!"

My lovely wife asks me, "Have you been gentle with yourself today?" Isn't that a beautiful way to remind me to love myself?

I remember a hymn I sang as a child:

---

38. Wikipedia, "Silent Generation."
39. Wikipedia, "Baby Boomers."

Musings

> "Jesus loves the little children
> All the children of the world;
> Red and yellow, black and white,
> *They are precious in his sight;*
>
> Jesus loves the little children of the world."[40]

You are precious. Be gentle with yourself.

Saved From the Monster

In the movie "*2001*," Hal the computer takes over the space ship. It was surreal watching the lone astronaut try to take back control of his life from a machine.

How controlled are we by our technology? Anyone can contact us "24/7". We are rarely out of reach of someone's beck and call. We depend on computers to communicate, research topics, and do price comparison shopping. We laugh along at funny jokes and videos. We shut out the world with ear buds.

There is a story of a king who had three sons. He sent the sons into the world to learn a skill. After four years they came back home. The king said, "What did you learn?" They took the king out to a clearing in the woods where a pile of bones lay. The first son said some words over the bones, and they came together to form a skeleton. The second son waved his hands over the skeleton, and it was covered with muscle, sinew, and skin. The third son blew breath into what was now an inert lion. It began to live. It then jumped on the king, and his three sons and devoured them.

Are we allowing technology to consume part of our spiritual being? Do we know that our drive for the most, the best and the cheapest supports child labor, sweat shops, and abuse of men and women in other countries, as well as our own? We have heard or seen on the news the working conditions in other countries. Is our obsession with technology the monster coming to consume us?

I am not suggesting we do away with our technology. Without it, you wouldn't likely be reading these musings. However, we can diminish technology's control by not upgrading each time there's a slightly different version. We can create quiet time for family and peace by cutting off our television, computer, cell phone, iPod, iPhone, and iPad. Take a techno

---

40. Wikipedia, "Woolston."

break for a few hours, a day or a weekend. Discover that life does not reside inside the world of Google.

My dog lets me know when I have spent enough time at the computer or television. She sits at my feet, looking at me. I feel her eyes. I try to ignore her. When she realizes that doesn't work, she "woofs" at me. "Hey, I am here. I need attention. I am more important than what you are doing. That thing you are so enamored with doesn't play, doesn't show love by licking your face, and doesn't bring you a leash so you can go for a walk to see and experience the sights and smells of the world."

I am saved from the techno-monster by a small furry bundle of intelligence and love! Have you noticed that *God* is the result of reverse spelling of the word *dog*?

Rabbits and Eggs??

I was somewhat precocious as a child, wanting to know how life worked. The questions seemed to have no end. I asked questions typical of a curious child. Why is the sky blue? How does the moon stay in the sky? Where do babies come from?

There were other situations that didn't make sense to me. When I asked about them, my parents had to do some serious thinking. Early on, I had serious thoughts about the practical aspects of a big fat man coming down a chimney, especially when the flue was closed. Where were the wings on the reindeer? Why were we creating fear and mayhem on October 31st? What holds that heavy airplane up in the air?

The strangest one to me was the idea of a rabbit hiding eggs. Rabbits don't produce eggs, much less hide things! Even if the rabbit got the eggs from the chickens, on the farm I never saw a chicken lay anything but brown and white eggs. Would an Easter Squirrel make more sense? At least they hide nuts. But of course they don't lay eggs so more thought is needed!

Most of the fun in Easter egg hunts was in how many you could find. The search was often frantic, as the one with the most eggs won a prize. The core to some of my clients' neuroses could involve finding very few or, even worse, never finding any eggs. This lack of success in egg-hunting may have led some to a career as a corporate raider. You know the saying, "The one with the most toys wins!"

I declare a new campaign to vote the rabbit out of office, and elect the Easter Squirrel until something better comes along! There are always more nuts than eggs so everyone can get a fair share. There is no need for trauma to anyone's self-worth.

What Matters in the End?

As most of you have heard by now, Mike Wallace, the legendary newsman, died on Saturday, April 7, 2012 at 93. I find very revealing his son's statement about what his father remembered as his mental state deteriorated:

> " . . . The interesting thing is, he never mentions the TV program he co-anchored, "60 Minutes." It's as if it didn't exist. It's as if that part of his memory is completely gone. The only thing he really talks about is family—me, my kids, my grandkids, his great-grandchildren. There's a lesson there. This is a man who had a fabulous career, and for whom work always came first. Now he can't even remember it."[41]

We spend most of our lives giving our time and energy to our jobs and professions. When greeting someone, the first question we usually ask is, "What do you do?" or "What kind of work are you in?" Even with close friends, we rarely spend time asking them what is important to them, what they believe about life, or the kinds of questions that reveal their spirit.

We focus our energy to make our work the top priority in our lives. In the end, is that really what is most important? What we do for a living is an important part of life. Our work makes a big contribution to our lives and to the lives of others if we do it with integrity and compassion. However, if we focus on work to the exclusion of everything else, haven't we missed the soul of living?

Maybe our work contributes most to life when we bring our love of family, our faith, and our awareness and love of God's creation into it.

Jesus said, "Enter through the narrow gate. For wide is the gate and broad is the road that leads to destruction, and many enter through it. But small is the gate and narrow the road that leads to life, and only a few find it." (Matt 7:13–14)

I feel he is asking me to focus on those things that represent the true beauty of life: believing in a loving and compassionate God, loving ourselves, loving family and friends, and accepting love in return.

It's never too late to find the "narrow gate" that leads to life.

41. Fox, "Record."

Religious Superiority

When a group claims their belief is *"the"* religion, they are in danger of excluding any of God's children who don't fit into their mold. In fact, they can push others away with unrelenting zeal.

Religious, political or any fanatics for that matter, allow no room for anyone else's point of view. Nor do they honor a person who has differing beliefs. How boring and frightening it would be, if we all believed the same thing! Different points of view open us to new possibilities.

I see all people as creations of the Spiritual Presence, First Mover, and Author of Life? The media grabs hold with gusto to the actions of extremists. Hearing so many bad things about others, we can be conditioned toward a prejudiced view of other religions or belief systems. While many radicals rant and distort specific texts of whatever book they base their beliefs on, I expect many of their followers are reasonable, loving people. We don't often get the chance to share beliefs.

Are we still living out the belief of Greek mythology that there are a number of gods who do battle to control life? "My god is bigger than your god!" "I am going to heaven and you are going to hell!" Maybe there needs to be a new classification in the Diagnostic and Statistic Manual for Mental Disorders: *"Narcissistic Religious Superiority Disorder[NRSD]"*!

During my religious upbringing, I was told that there are many "gods" and many "lords," but there is only one God, the Source of all things and life. Those of us who profess to be Christian can be prone to NRSD if we believe that God is only a Christian God.

Could it be that God has many messengers? We might consider the possibility that God is the hub or center of the wheel of Creation which has many spokes, ways, and messengers leading to the Center. Most of us were taught that Jesus is God's son, his primary messenger. Could there be other messengers from God in our lives? Tolerance and inclusiveness are parts of all belief systems that are based on love and unity.

We may do well to seek out those who frighten us or repulse us, rather than walking on the opposite side of the street. We may learn much if we ask them to share what they believe so we can attempt to understand who they are. Our worldview may be expanded even if our beliefs remain the same.

The Power of Touch

We need water, food, and protection from the elements. This is the first level of the hierarchy developed by the psychologist Abraham Maslow outlining our needs. He says these are the basic needs that must be met before we can move to the next level.

We have a fundamental need for touch. Maslow may imply it later on in his writing. If our need for touch is not satisfied early on, we may not survive. In the previous century hospitals discovered that when the nurseries were insufficiently staffed, the children who were left in the bassinets and untouched for hours after birth, became very ill or died. In orphanages a majority of babies largely left alone died before they were seven months old. (There are a number of articles supporting this now.)[42] We live in a culture that often is afraid to touch, to get close to other human beings. The sales in antibacterial hand lotion have skyrocketed. We've become a nation of "germaphobes."[43] Some are saying we are becoming more susceptible to illness by sanitizing too much. We don't give our bodies enough chance to build antibodies.

In Europe, people not only hug when they meet, but also kiss on each cheek. They may not have developed the paranoia about getting too close to each other as we have, but touch is important to them.

We have only to look at animals and how they groom their young. It is a beautiful and heartwarming experience to watch an animal mother attend to her young, and watch other animals roll, play, and chew on each other. Maybe that is one reason God created animals, to remind us of the importance of touch and loving togetherness.

Safe tactile stimulation—shaking hands, hugging—with another person can feed our souls, and can let us know we are alive and grounded. It tells us we are worthy of time and attention, confirming we belong to the "pack."

I have been told we need three hugs a day to feel alive and healthy. I would go even further. Even though we may have gotten our three hugs, I give you permission to cheat and say you haven't had all three yet. Get a few more hugs? That's never a bad thing.

Don't be afraid to ask for hugs from those that you feel safe in receiving a hug!

42. Servo, Tom, "Infants."
43. *Urban Dictionary*, "germaphobes."

Powerful Words

Two of my favorite words are tenacity and resourcefulness.

We live in a world of entitlement. Too many feel entitled to getting the best of everything. Often their sense of entitlement doesn't include putting much effort to obtain what they want. "Just give it to me."

Entitlement is a deceptively shiny stone that weighs us down with apathy.

My grandfather gave me my first job when I was six years old. He grew tomato plants in his greenhouse. He taught me how to package them. We would take several sheets of newspaper, place the tomato plants in the middle, then take a hand full of mud that he had mixed from topsoil, and place the mud on the roots of the plants. He showed me how to fold the newspaper so the tops of the plants would stick out and not be crushed. I was given the responsibility of carrying them to the local hardware store, and carried them with the greatest of care. He would pay me a percentage of the sales. This first job implanted the early seeds of my tenacity, an "unwilling to accept defeat or stop doing or having something."[44] I also became resourceful, learning how to deal with new situations and solve problems.

What a world we live in! We have everything we need not only to survive, but also to experience exciting adventures. The resources are infinite. We need to develop the tenacity to look around, to search, and to use our discoveries in a way that brings about a creative solution. All that will give us a sense of accomplishment.

After all, we are created in the image of our Creator, a Presence that is steadfast, provides us with resources, and trusts us to use these resources in creative and positive ways. He gave us the gifts of tenacity and resourcefulness. From the beginning, we are told, "Then God blessed them, and said "Be fruitful and increase in number; Fill the earth and subdue it . . . " (Gen 1: 28a) However, this certainly doesn't say to me, "Take all you can and ignore the consequences."

We have a tremendous Power behind us to help us "keep on keeping on" and we have the resources to learn tenacity and resourcefulness toward creative and responsible ends.

---

44. Cambridge, "tenacity."

Musings

Living Responsibly

We can talk to our television sets or newspapers or gather in groups to grouse about the poor conditions of the world and idly blame the President and Congress for our problems. We are great at offering armchair solutions. We have become experts in "talking the talk." And as Dr. Phil would say, "And how's that working for you?"

One who did very little talking was Mahatma Gandhi. He said, "Be the change." He lived his life "being the change," and two nations responded.

As a Boy Scout we were asked to not only repeat the Scout Oath and the Scout Law, but also to put them into practice at all times. We were asked and helped to leave a camp site better than we found it. Look up the Scout Oath and the Scout Law. They are both about leaving a beautiful trail, literally, and metaphorically.

Is the trail we leave in our journey better than we found it? Or in our race to do all and get what we think we have to have, are we leaving any trails of destruction? Is our wake more similar to that of a tornado or are we seen as the caretakers we were asked to be in the beginning?

We have ample opportunity to make a mark that has a ripple effect around the planet. We can recycle, support local business, spend no more than we make, support only non-violent entertainment and responsible charities, and become a "Good Samaritan" to those in need. We can also be active in making our government and corporations accountable for their actions.

Yes, it takes time, forethought and effort. I have to make a trip to the dump with the garbage, and then another trip to the recycling center. At the latter, I separate the glass, cardboard, paper, and plastic into separate bins. These are small stones in the pond that create ripples that affect people around the shoreline.

God's creation and gift of life is a canvas of utmost beauty. We have been entrusted to handle the canvas of this Artist with the greatest of care.

Look behind you. How does the path look?

Refreshing Honesty

Sometimes we go to church and put on a face of piety. There is an old saying, "Putting on our Sunday-go-to-meeting clothes." We appear to be sincere. Should we ask ourselves a few questions from time to time? "Are we being honest with who we are and what we are feeling? "Do we continue to profess, at times, what we do not feel? Would people be appalled if we were to say, "I don't believe in God today?" Or "I have doubts about the physical resurrection of Jesus, not to mention the birth of a baby without the joining of a sperm and an egg." Or, "I really feel lost and lonely today."

Growing up with a minister father, I frequently saw people stand up during a service confessing a personal struggle, and requesting prayer. They gave heartfelt testimonials about their faith. There was childlike trust that it was okay to speak of the communion of believers.

If we truly profess to be followers of Jesus, then we are accepting and compassionate to everyone, no matter what their thoughts about life.

Is your church a safe place to be, to express your doubts and share differences? The honesty in Bible stories can be somewhat threatening. They include "the good, the bad, and the ugly."

I love the honesty of the man in the Bible who told Jesus, "I do believe, help me overcome my unbelief." (Mark 9:24) Sounds like he was having some struggles with his beliefs and faith! One of my favorite quotes from M. Scott Peck in *The Road Less Traveled* says "Holiness is in questioning everything."[45]

Our challenge is to be honest with where we are in the moment, in the light of God's total acceptance. And we have to be discerning about who we share with. Jesus spoke to this about what we do with our pearls. (Matt 7:6)

One Sunday as I was greeting people leaving worship, I asked a pregnant woman how she was feeling. Her response to her minister on Sunday after worship was not what one would expect. She blurted out her true feelings at the moment. "I feel like s__t!" she said. After the initial shock, I thought, how refreshing that is from the routine, "Good sermon, preacher."

Are we being honest with ourselves? Do we have a community of believers we can share that honesty with?

Embodiment of Hate

We may be very free in making this kind of statement: "I hate doing this," "I hate my job," "I hate what you have done," or all too frequently, "I hate you."

Are we justifying the use of this forceful and negative term, "hate" by saying we need to make frequent distinctions between good and evil?

---

45. Peck, *Road*, 193.

Musings

Do we believe that addressing evil by using the word "hate" is to separate ourselves from it?

I think just the opposite happens. If we express and feel negativity in using the term "hate," we can embody hate. We justify violence as redemptive. Many hate the Muslims, the Afghans, and Al-Qaida and justify it by saying they hate us. The killing fields lie between these two negative forces of evil. Nobody wins!

The only way to stand against evil is through forgiveness and inclusion.

"He drew a circle that shut me out —
Heretic, rebel, a thing to flout.
But Love and I had the wit to win:
We drew a circle that took him in."[46]

Surely there are ways to approach people with differing beliefs and religions other than to annihilate them. Maybe I am a dreamer and naïve when dealing with people who are indoctrinated to hate. Jesus said as it is written in Matt 5: 43-44, "You have heard that it was said, 'Love your neighbor and hate your enemy.' But I tell you, *love your enemies* and pray for those who persecute you...."

Maybe we can start a groundswell of compassionate energy by attempting to understand why certain groups hate us, learning to love them as children of God, and praying for them. If we can substitute love and prayer when we feel hate, we can make a difference, not only in the lives of those we are trying to love but in our own lives.

The Unbearable Lightness of Being

I have taken this topic from a 1988 motion picture of the same name. It is a deeply confusing movie, and may not have the same meaning I am attributing to it. I can identify with the unbearable lightness to just being. Maybe I am borrowing from Existential Philosophy that basically says the essential core of our being lies in our existence.

Our lives can become heavy with the amount of things we collect, worries about what we need to survive, things from the past that drag us down, and other earthly baggage. Many of us create drama, problems, and action to feel like we matter. When we experience moments of the lightness of just being, people often say, "Just pinch me so that I know I am not

---

46. Markham, American Author, 1852 to 1940.

dreaming." Why the pinch? To bring us back down to earth with a moment of pain. There is enough pain as it is. Why not enjoy the lightness?

Paul says: "It is for freedom that Christ has set us free. Stand firm, then, and do not let yourselves be burdened again by a yoke of slavery." (Gal 5:1) Have we become slaves to the things with which we surround ourselves? Being burdened by such mental and physical weight leaves little room for light or lightness. It takes a great deal of courage to experience being.

"Just being" is noticing where we are right now. We are no longer encumbered by the past or future, the worries of surviving, or people's opinion of us. We experience the freedom of being the observer of the moment. It is like being lifted from the ground and just floating, like those flying dreams some of us have.

However, we fear that if we enjoy life with some sense of abandon, we will lose control. But whoever said we had control in the first place? It is an illusion we live with, even though we are reminded daily that the outcome of life is not in our control.

Jesus says, "Your eye is the lamp of your body. When your eyes are healthy, your whole body also is full of light. But when they are unhealthy, your body also is full of darkness." (Luke 11)

Experience the lightness of the moment. Don't worry. We have landing gears and will always touch down to the ground again.

Then Face To Face

    This park bench has become a throne for my spirit
    My court is ready and waiting to serve my soul
    A very small but powerful musician sits above me
    Graciously pouring out its heart in song
    That begins to soothe the tormented beast
    The feathered fans of attending winds
    Caress the sweated brow
    The scents of earth's kitchen fill my spirit
    With soothing memories of more peaceful times
    The drama unfolding before me
    Carries my soul back to childlike wonder
    My soul does see face to face
    As my body looks through the glass darkly

The Law of Three

Are there angels or messengers that nudge us in directions that are important to our lives? Do they subtly attempt to make us aware of things that will help us in life? I don't know about you, but there have been times in my life when I literally looked over my shoulder to see if someone was there. It was like an invisible presence was nearby. No, I do not hallucinate, but I do feel like there has been some quantum shift in the moment.

To be aware of those times I need to take a closer look, I developed "The Law of Three." If something happens three times, I pay attention.

Here are some examples:

- I have heard a book title mentioned. I see it discussed on television. After I have forgotten about the first two incidences, I will be in a book store and the book practically jumps off the shelf at me.

- I have a dream about someone I haven't seen in years. In conversation someone mentions the person. While reading, I am reminded again of this person.

Some would say these are just some of life's coincidences. I don't believe in coincidence. There may be more to the experiences that come our way than initially meets the eye. In the thesaurus, "coincidence" is also called "providence."[47] Providence is defined as God's guidance.

God moves in mysterious ways. A lot of times we are too busy to pay attention. Using The Law of Three", I buy the book. I try to contact the person and ask them how they are doing. What I find is usually very timely, surprising or enlightening.

Develop your own method to become aware of the presence and messages from the realm "beyond the curtain."

The "Law of Three" works for me.

Going with the Flow

I look forward to summertime and lying on a float in the lake. There is peace in floating and slowly spinning as I drink in the mountains, trees, and water around me. Time no longer matters. I am fed by the energy and beauty around me. I watch the dazzling facets of color on a dragonfly alighting upon my toe. The water bug skates across the water, easing my tension

---

47. Thesaurus.com. "coincidence."

and worries. There are no "have tos," "got tos," "oughts," or "shoulds" in those moments.

We need to learn the healing art of doing nothing. Maybe the peace and quiet frightens us because our lives are so full of activity. We walk into our home and flip on the television. We get into our automobiles and turn on the radio. In groups everyone talks at the same time. Our poor attempt to shut out the world is to place speaker buds in our ears, creating more noise. "Sit there. *Don't* just do something" would sound strange to our ears.

To me, the destination is not as important as the journey. The journey teaches. The destination is another line drawn through our to-do list.

I love fairy tales and myths. They teach us about life and our choices, good and bad. I remember a particular scene when a prince tries to find a cure for his father's illness. A poor beggar along the way tries to get the prince's attention. The prince was in such a hurry to find the healing potion that he practically ran over the old beggar, shouting, "Get out of my way!" And he rushed on. Unknown to the prince, the beggar was a spirit guide with knowledge of how to get the healing potion.

Time is an illusion created by the mechanical and now, the digital clock. Before clocks people went by the cycles of the sun and moon as well as the seasons of nature. There was less urgency.

We may need to learn to "go with the flow". It could be part of our own "healing potion."

> You don't have to row
> See the beauty in being slow
> Now you are in the know
> Ah, you begin to glow
>
> —Edward L. Boye, 2013

There is a realm beyond this common and practical ground we all walk daily. It is a spiritual place. When I say *spiritual*, I am not limiting myself to the religious.

Beyond the Obvious

Are we aware of the energy around us? Our bodies and brains produce a tremendous amount of physical energy. Some of that energy can be measured with CAT or PET scans, MRIs, EEGs, EKGs, or other technology.

Musings

And yet, there is a realm of spiritual energy around us that can't be measured by machines. We *can* experience its presence.

People believe talking to their plants makes them grow bigger, better, and more fruitful. Some empirical purists scoff at this. My mother had many house plants and watered, fertilized, touched, and talked to them. She had large, succulent and brightly colored flowering plants. Something more than watering and fertilizing was going on there.

There is a tremendous power in being aware of our spiritual energy. Negative words and thoughts can scar the ground we walk on. It's like we're a machine with whirling blades, cutting a path of destruction, and destroying ourselves. Negative energy breeds negative results.

We have a choice. We can focus on sending out positive vibrations. Our body literally pulsates with joy, love, creativity, and other building blocks when we are in this positive state of being. It doesn't come easy. Sometimes we literally have to throw our hands up and shout, "*stop*" to cut off negative thoughts.

There are many methods for getting in touch with our gifts of positive creativity: meditation, prayer, mantras, and emptying our minds with thought-stopping when we engage in destructive thinking. Using these tools of being, thinking and acting positively helps them come natural. It is all too easy to give in to those places of darkness.

Balance

Balance is the ability of an object to stay steady while resting on a small object. Given the number of square inches under our feet and the weight of our body on those feet, standing upright is a miracle. But even more, we can lean, run, spin, and still stay upright. We take our ability to stay balanced for granted.

We are bodies of energy. We spend most of our time expending that energy through action or thought. Acting and thinking are one side of the balance of living. In order to have balance we also need to pay attention to the other side of the scale, retreating, withdrawing, detaching, and spending minimal amounts of energy.

"If only I had more time" we often say or think. When we wish for more time, it is not really to do more things, but a cry for rest from our endeavors. There is a deep desire in our frantic expenditure of energy to stop, sit down, lie down, retreat or withdraw from the pressing demands for our time. Some of us create excessive demands on our time from fear that we will not be accepted, respected or loved unless we accomplish certain tasks.

We cannot put the accelerator of an automobile to the floor and leave it there without eventually blowing up the engine or wrecking the car. The same is true of our bodies. When we blow our "engine," we have heart attacks, strokes or breakdown of other body parts.

We do have an ideal role model. However, we probably miss out on this part of his life because we focus on his actions on earth. A popular acronym is: WWJD ("What Would Jesus Do"). Reading the Bible recently, I was suddenly struck by how many times he withdrew from the action. He began his ministry by retreating for forty days. He withdrew when John was imprisoned (Matt 4:12), then again when John was beheaded. (Matt 14:13) He withdrew after feeding five thousand (Matt 14:23), and also after praying in the garden at Gethsemane. (Mark14:32) Luke says in 5:16, "But Jesus often withdrew to lonely places and prayed." He did this to get away from the crowd's expectations, and to renew his strength and spirit.

Society gives us kudos for productivity. Jesus advises us to do many things in his name, but he also set the example that one needs to balance action with times of retreat for prayer, contemplation, and rest.

You have permission to retreat often, given by the Author of life.

Truly Rich

Most of us have a narrow view of riches. We often think of riches in dollar signs—finding a lost Van Gogh in the attic, inheriting from a rich aunt or winning the lottery. We long for big houses, luxury cars and yachts, exotic trips around the world, first class seating, and on and on. We believe if we have these things, we will be rich.

The other day, I heard an interview of a person with such riches. He is a well known movie star and owns an island with a yacht and full crew on standby. During the interview he was with guests and obviously unhappy, yelling and screeching. Is he rich? I think, "Not, really." I wouldn't trade places with him and his torment, even if it included his fame and all that he owns.

I came across a quote that really struck me: "The richest person is not the one who has the most, but the one who needs the least."[48] How

---

48. Anonymous.

freeing that sounds! I do believe we have been brainwashed by advertising. I believe the line between need and want has been blurred.

I visited a church member one day years ago. He was an old farmer living in a small clapboard house on about two acres of land. He had a garden out back. It was obvious that he didn't have much more than what I have described. His wife had died a year or two before. He lived alone, and we sat in rocking chairs on the front porch. He was in his old bib overalls, talking about life. Suddenly, he wrapped his arms around himself in a hug, twisting back and forth, laughing joyfully. He said, "Preacher, the Good Maaaaster has been good to me." I have never sensed such a genuine sense of satisfaction and peace in someone who had so little.

Well, the "Good Maaaaster" has told us what is valuable and how our hearts can be affected by what we treasure.

An Enchanting Story

One type of speed reading is when you focus your eyes down the middle of the page, catching only the core of the story and eliminating extra words as unimportant. Are we often running down the middle of the page of our lives in a hurry to get to the next chapter? Living like this may cause us to finish "our book" sooner than we want!

One of my favorite leisure activities is reading. (I was going to say "pastimes", but realized that I don't want just to pass time. I want to experience the whole story!) Reading for me is an immersion in the story. It gives me the ability to travel to other worlds and live other lives. The adjectives, adverbs, associations, and analogies are vivid colors in a world the author is painting.

Without the minor details, there would be less excitement in life. We would be jumping from one activity to the next, one page to the next, without really living. We have been conditioned to pay attention only to the headlines, the sensational.

Matthew 6:34 says "Therefore do not worry about tomorrow, for tomorrow will worry about itself. Each day has enough trouble of its own." This often helps me in stopping negative thoughts about the future.

Contemplate a line from the television soap opera, *Days of Our Lives*: "Like the sands through an hour glass, so are the days of our lives." It sounds almost boring, unless you take time to be enchanted by each grain of sand.

Immerse yourself in today's story. You may find that it is more fascinating than you think!

Respecting Our Elders

I am fascinated by the Old West and the rich Native American culture. They learned to live with the land and respect it. They adapted to the environment and seasons with no attempt to change or control the natural flow of life. They honored and respected the elders. Often the chief and older leaders in the tribe moved from leadership roles to being holy ones, offering wisdom and honor. People would gather in the meeting lodge and there would be respectful silence. Slowly the elder would begin telling a story.

Have we have forgotten the elderly in the wake of a youth culture? We use terms like, "He has been put out to pasture." I like the serenity of a pasture but I'm not interested in spending my day being ignored and chewing cud like an old bull.

Our elderly are an incredible source of wisdom and experience. They carry on the oral tradition. They have information you cannot find in books. We can feel the dancing fire of the spirit as they tell a story.

Wikipedia offers this definition about the American Indian elder:

> "*The Elder:* Not all old or elderly people are considered elders. An elder is a person that has accumulated a great deal of wisdom and knowledge throughout his or her lifetime, especially in the tradition and customs of the group. Elders emphasize listening and not asking *why*. There isn't any word in the Cree language for "why." A learner must sit quietly and patiently while the elder passe[s] on *their* wisdom. Listening is considered to be very important. Questions were not encouraged . . . questions *were* considered rude. . . . Learners were also encouraged to watch and listen to what was happening around them. Eventually with enough patience and enough time the answer would come to the learner. When this happened, the learning was truly his *[or her]* own."[49]

Asking "why" in the midst of storytelling breaks the mystical flow of the story. Often, if the listener maintains patience, questions will be answered by the end of the telling.

Have you ever taken time to sit down and listen to the stories of an older person? Have you seen aliveness and excitement dance in their eyes?

---

49. Wikipedia, "Elders."

Musings

They may tell a story you have heard often. Maybe this is good, because it can teach us to listen. Each moment we listen, we can be transported to a different world. And more often than not, we learn something.

Create time to tell the stories of your life. For those listening, it will be a magic carpet ride!

Que, Sera, Sera

My aunt had a RCA Victrola and a stack of 12" 78 rpm vinyl records. There was one in particular I loved: "Que, Sera, Sera" sung by Doris Day. I wore out the grooves on that record. (Oh, I do date myself!) I am not sure what my attraction to that particular song was at such a young age. When I listened to it, I felt a sense that everything was going to be all right.

Que, Sera, Sera, "whatever will be, will be," is an inexact translation of Spanish or Italian. [50] What a way to look at life! "Whatever will be, will be!" It suggests that we have no control over what happens. We can only be responsible for how we respond.

Yet we spend a lot of time trying to control our lives, using a wide variety of resources, some reliable, some not so reliable. Is there a consistent, trustworthy, and authentic source that can teach us to live this journey we are on?

There is a story about the life of one who lived over two thousand years ago that may fill that need. Shouldn't we pay attention to the life of someone who continues to have a major influence and presence in life for over two thousand years? Can we learn ways that will help us survive the overwhelming stimulus of our lives and contribute to life being a better experience for all?

Dictionaries change. Encyclopedias change. The internet changes every second. But the basic foundation of this source has never changed over the past two thousand years.

Think about it!

Joy

We miss the joy of what is happening right now when we anticipate the worst. We lose awareness of the aliveness of the moment when we spend a

---

50. Wikipedia, "Que, Sera, Sera."

time reviewing worst-case scenarios. We miss experiencing life with all of our senses when we fill our heads with "what ifs." Perhaps we fear the pain of disappointment. "There's going to be a great parade in town. And with my luck, it'll probably rain." It is just another way of feeling we have control of life. If we anticipate the worst, we think it will make the pain less intense.

We know life is going to happen, so why worry about it? Staying in a constant state of "worst-case scenarios" can lead to negative outcomes. We aren't comfortable around people who paint a dark picture. If we agree negative thinking can influence our life outcomes, it stands to reason positive thinking can also make a difference.

Enjoy the experience of the moment. Take time to really look around. Capture the nuances of what's around you. Think the best. Enjoy the experience, even when you crash into the hard wall of reality. Just say, "Oh, well, what a grand opportunity to learn something new!" This is very difficult to do in the midst of pain, but when we are able, we can have at least moments where we can shift our thinking.

Joy is more than experiencing pleasure. Pleasure is usually short-lived. We can take great pleasure in eating a bowl of rich vanilla or chocolate ice cream. The dictionary says joy is "feelings of great happiness or pleasure, especially of an elevated or spiritual kind."[51] Joy helps us transcend the earthly experience. It is more than momentary delight.

We have a choice to create joy for ourselves and others, or we can "drown the parade" with negative rainfall. I try to remember this short poem: "Two men look through the same prison bars: one sees the mud and one the stars."[52]

Celebrity Status

How do you want to be perceived by others: by your work, how you act, how much money you have, where you live, the car you drive, and the trips you brag about taking? We want to feel good about who we are. We want to feel like we count. We want to feel distinct and unique.

There was a man some two thousand years ago who told all of us that we have a light to shine, a gift of life to give, and a love to share. We were told to do it quietly, without fanfare. How many times did Jesus tell his disciples and the people he healed not to tell anyone? He didn't need celebrity

---

51. Microsoft Encarta, "joy."
52. Langbridge, American Author, 1849 to 1922.

status. He didn't need applause, trophies, plaques, or certificates. He didn't want to be written up in *Entertainment Weekly* magazine. He said the reward would come later.

The older I get, the less I see value in promoting myself. Give of your talents quietly. Doing it quietly says a lot about your motivation.

Celebrity stars fade. They can be imprinted in a sidewalk for people to walk over, wear down, spit on, and crush cigarette butts on.

I have come to one conclusion about self-worth, personal importance, and what life is all about. We don't have to work so hard to impress others. Each of us already has status. Besides what difference will it make for others to think you and I are above the rest of humanity?

"Whoever wants to be my disciple, must deny themselves and take up their cross and follow me." (Matt16:24) He is not suggesting we be a martyr or doormat. He is saying to deny that part of you that is self-serving. Avoid the temptation to put yourself on a pedestal. Why would anyone want to do that anyway? You can fall off and break your neck. Besides, it is lonely up there!

The *Internet* is a Lonely Hunter

The May 2012 issue of *The Atlantic Magazine* says, "Social media—from Facebook to Twitter—has made us more densely networked than ever. Yet, for all this connectivity, new research suggests that we have never been lonelier (or more narcissistic) and that this loneliness is making us mentally and physically ill."[53] Our addictive use of social media sites has made us more accessible, yet we are often stuck in the self-imposed isolation of our LCD and LED screens.

Test results show that loneliness creates more stress hormones in our body. Loneliness is not just in the brain as a condition of thinking. It affects every cell in our body.

Social networking creates a false sense of intimacy. I even have some resistance to talking on the telephone. Being face to face creates an experience of total communication. We can feel the spirit of the other person, see deep into their eyes, watch their body language and facial expressions, and feel the energy radiate between us.

When people share their successes, beautiful pictures, and videos that go viral on social networks, how do you feel? Some may say, "Why can't my

---

53. Marche, "Lonely," *Atlantic*, 2012.

life be as good?" Others feel like victims of their circumstances and become depressed. Many get pleasure from seeing others flourish, and express gratitude for what they have to offer. Often it motivates us to try something new. It is not the social networks that cause loneliness. We can use our brain. We are responsible for using the technology that has been created.

We lost something when American architecture stopped including wrap around front porches. Those porches were a great example of social networking. People would sit in their rocking chairs in the evening. Others strolling down the sidewalk would be invited to sit and visit awhile. This is not just my nostalgia. It's reference to a time when we weren't isolated by computer screens, television sets, iPhones, and iPods. Sharing, communication and intimacy occurred on those porches.

The word "twitter" means "to talk in a quick, informal way about unimportant things . . . to utter successive chirping sounds."[54] Does this suggest that the communication is the result of "bird brain" or small-brain thinking?

Human interaction can be "messy". We often don't like to look at the rawness of life. We bypass having to face the "messiness" by creating a persona on a liquid crystal diode. We can exit any time we feel uncomfortable or at a loss for loving and creative expression.

The old hymn says it best:

> "Blest be the tie that binds
> Our hearts in Christian *(or any kind of)* love;
> The fellowship of kindred minds
> Is like to that above.
> We share each other's woes,
> Our mutual burdens bear;
> And often for each other flows
> The sympathizing tear."[55]

A Singing Heart

When someone uses the term "minister," we usually think of the pastor of a church. Popular thinking includes the individual being "called" (feel a spiritual inspiration). Many also believe ministers need a seminary degree.

---

54. *Merriam-Webster*, "twitter."
55. Fawcett D.D., Theologian, 1739 to 1817.

Musings

Limiting or restricting ourselves to these narrow definitions means missing what Jesus said over and over, not just in words but also through action. He chose twelve men, some of them considered rough characters. They had no seminary training, and he told them to go out and minister to the sick, afflicted, imprisoned, widowed and orphaned.

Being "called" doesn't apply just to a full time religious profession. We are all "called" to do something in this life. What is your calling--law, landscaping, politics, law enforcement, teach, or "household engineering"? Paul tells us, "Whatever you do, work at it with all your heart, as working for the Lord, not for human masters . . . ." (Col. 3:23) Whatever our choice of work, we can do it as a calling with love, integrity, and honesty.

Most of us have programming to reach out, be compassionate and to pursue ways to connect with others. Jesus calls us to minister to one another. All of us are here for a purpose and to make a difference.

The reward in giving is the feeling that we have made a difference in someone's life and that we have opened our hearts to love. There is no better gift than to see gratitude in someone's eyes and feel it in their spirit when they receive this kind of love.

I received a wonderful surprise of love recently when I had been sick for several weeks with bronchitis. Friends brought me dinner. And gourmet it was! I felt a warm feeling of being connected and loved. I wanted to spread that caring and compassion to others.

When people question me about what they can do with their lives, I ask "What makes your heart sing?" We are all here to minister in whatever job or profession we are led to. A singing heart is much better than one that is discordant.

Encompassing Differences

Do you march to the beat of an "unconventional" drum like I do? I enjoy being different and challenging the "shoulds" of life. I detest pretension, the fancy cloak that often covers the nakedness of truth.

And yet, we need to look in the mirror at our own actions and protestations, lest we be victims of our own self-righteousness. Jesus spoke to this when he said, "Why do you look at the speck of sawdust in your brother's eye and pay no attention to the plank in your own eye?" (Matt 7:3) Many point out "that which we dislike in others may be what we dislike about ourselves."

When we are able to accept that we "hide" both good and not so good truths inside ourselves, we will be less critical of others, and more willing to hear their truth. We will not feel as compelled that they must change. As a result, they often become more willing to connect with us.

I admit that I have "dropped a name or two" to make myself seem more seem important. I have been so insecure about myself that I have tried to talk others out of their feelings and perspective on life. It doesn't work. It has only created tension and distance from other people. Everyone wants to be respected for their beliefs and ways of dealing with life.

Honoring another person for who they are (their feelings, opinions and choices), is one of the greatest gifts we can give someone.

Accepting differences is to see the rainbow of humanity.

Life Can Be Messy

I have told this story for years and was recently reminded of it. It speaks about procrastination, predicament, discernment, courage, risk, fear, and being a victim. It is about life and choices. We have all been there.

There was a little bird in Central Park in New York City. It was October and he was playing around in the leaves. Suddenly, he realized he heard no other birds because they had already flown south. So he started flying. By the time he was over Pennsylvania it was so cold his wings began to freeze. He started falling as he could no longer fly. He was over a farm and fell right into the cow lot. A cow had just passed and made its daily "deposit." The little bird landed right in the middle of it which cushioned his fall. It was warm and his wings began to thaw. He was so happy. He had been saved. As he lay there he thought, "If I try to fly again the same thing might happen and I might not be so lucky. The next time I could hit the ground and die." So he decided to just lie there in the warmth and started "twittering" a song of joy. A passing cat heard the bird "twittering", and came to investigate. Following the sound, the cat discovered the bird and enjoyed a small meal.

Morals of the story:

1. *Not everyone who dumps on you is your enemy.*
2. *Not everyone who gets you out of crap is your friend.*
3. *And when you're in deep do-do, it's best to keep your mouth shut!*

Musings

Also, I might add:

4. *Be careful when and where you "twitter".*

Doubt

Conservative and fundamental religious beliefs often allow no room for doubt. Doubt is seen as something that plays with our minds and saps our faith. When doubt is denied, it only grows larger and leads to fear. Those who fear doubt work all the harder to deny its existence.

M. Scott Peck, in his book *The Road Less Traveled*, says "The path to holiness lies through questioning *everything*."[56] I like what Clarence Darrow said, the lawyer of the Scopes trial about teaching evolution in schools: "Just think of the tragedy of teaching children not to doubt."[57] A questioning mind is a gift from our Creator. It is through the process of questioning that we gain wisdom and learn responsibility.

It is human to doubt. It keeps us sane. It causes us to look at life on a deeper level rather than accept the word of a perceived "authority." "Where there is doubt, faith has a reason for being." [58] When there are questions without answers, all that is left is faith. Paul probably defined it best when he said, "Now faith is confidence in what we hope for and assurance about what we do not see." (Heb 1:1)

This is a difficult concept to grasp in a world that values observable evidence. I like doubt. If we are determined, doubt will cause us to keep searching, learning, and discovering. A nineteenth century author said, "Doubt is the beginning, not the end, of wisdom."[59] When we have run out of trails to follow, we can hold on to hope and trust the assurance of what we cannot see.

You have likely had times when you doubted your faith. I certainly have. Even with all of our questions, we can return to faith and avoid a perpetual state of hopelessness. That is a dark and lonely place to be. I would rather gamble on hope for the assurance that this whole journey makes sense.

---

56. Peck, "Road," 193.
57. Darrow, American Lawyer, 1857 to 1938.
58. Taylor, *Certainty*, 81.
59. Author Unknown.

Kissing Frogs!

One of my childhood thrills was the arrival of the next Dell comic book. *Superman, Batman, Donald Duck, Goofy and Scrooge McDuck* were some of my favorite ones. Every once in a while, a comic book would adapt a Grimm's fairy tale.

The story that puzzled me most was *The Frog Prince*. You remember the story. The princess lost her golden ball in a pond and a frog retrieved it. But before he would give it to her, she had to promise to take him home. She agreed, but then ran off when he gave her the ball. The story ends with her kissing the frog and him turning into a handsome prince.

I could never quite buy that a princess would kiss a frog. Besides, I was always told that I would get warts from playing with frogs. But I wasn't sure this was true as I did play with frogs and never got warts.

Walt Disney, bless his soul, wanted to clean up the Grimm brothers' view of things. If you get a copy of the original *Grimm's Fairy Tales* and read *The Frog Prince*, we find out that Miss Princess was too repulsed (or too spoiled) to kiss a frog. What actually happened? She picked him up in disgust and splattered him against the castle wall! Then he turned into a handsome prince. I guess the stories were called "Grimm" for a reason![60]

Moral of the story: we really don't have to kiss frogs to find a prince or princess. Slamming someone against a wall is a bit extreme. However, we may feel that we have been slammed against a wall when others have been honest with us. Unfortunately, most of the time people aren't straightforward. Meeting someone who is frank can be a shock.

Too often we become victims. We give our power away. We allow others to intimidate, coerce, or seduce us into responding as they want us to. Yes, we need to keep our promises. The princess could have honored her promise to take the frog back to the castle. If she had respected him enough to be honest, perhaps she would have said "I will honor my promise and take you back to the castle, but I am not sleeping with you!" Perhaps her honesty would have broken the prince's spell as a frog.

Respect, honor, attention, and kindness can help a lot of unpleasant or disagreeable folk find the prince or princess within.

---

60. Grimm, "Frog."

Musings

The New Deity?

What do we need from a Higher Power? We need a reasonable explanation for the perplexities of life. We need a source that has the power to heal us. We need a belief in an ultimate authority that is awesome and mysterious. We need a source of security. Faith in God certainly embraces all of these.

When it comes down to it, don't we also turn to medical science for assurance? We want answers. This age of technology has allowed viral growth of new information that can make us feel more in control. We believe science has a cure so when we have an illness, we try everything we can. When there is a "magic pill" or procedure, we are awed at the mystery of it. We appreciate the knowledge and authority of the physician(s). Sometimes we act as if healthcare science is a new deity.

We are willing to put our loved ones through days, months, and sometimes years of existing without having much quality of life. We don't want to let go, and we believe science can save them. I personally have a *Certificate of Mental Peace* when it comes to this issue. My Living Will (and my Durable Power of Attorney for Healthcare) says I don't want anyone to take extra measures to keep me going when my situation is terminal.

In my first pastorate, I visited a ninety-four year-old member in a nursing home. She asked me, in a weary and hurting voice, "Preacher I am tired of living, but my children keep saying I will be all right. They want me keep going. Do you think God will condemn me for not wanting to continue living?" I said, "Ms. Barker, God loves us. You have lived a good and long life. When you are ready, God is always there to welcome you with open arms. Your children will grieve your leaving, but God will help them work through it." Two weeks later, I got a call that she had died. Sometimes people just need permission. I truly believe that we know at some level when our time is up.

Science has made our lives easier in many ways, and in many cases, has helped our quality of life as we are dying. Yet science doesn't fit all of the requirements we have for a deity. Science cannot walk with us or carry us when we need it. There is often no warmth in the sterile atmosphere of a lab or hospital. It cannot give us love and forgiveness. There may not be a soulful presence to give us the assurance we need. Science cannot promise us an eternal life.

Being sensitive to a dying person's needs could include options like providing peaceful music, beautiful pictures or scenes, or the reading of poetry and story-telling. The healing and soothing power of music, the human voice, touch, and spiritual presence can reunite the dying person with community and minimize their isolation in being "connected" to machines.

When my time comes, and I am not looking for it any time soon, I want to feel the presence of a Deity that will walk with me across the "wide divide." I hope to have a room full of family and friends to celebrate my bon voyage.

No Time To Reflect

How often do we think seriously, carefully, and calmly about our lives and the choices we make? We are so often inundated with stimuli that it can be like a carnival clown dodging baseballs.

We feel (and say) that we don't have time to do the things we think are needed. Time is a construct of humankind. I sometimes think we use clocks to push ourselves in living life faster than is healthy. Have you ever gone on a retreat or vacation, taken off your watch, and put away your phone? Did you feel less pressure to get somewhere or accomplish things?

We do have to make plans in order to survive. Yet, we don't have to allow our watches or phone to dictate our actions. I like the statement, "I am going to set aside some time to . . . . " Set aside time? Wow! Can we do that? We must "set time to the side" if we are going to experience reflection (careful thought), meditation (emptying the mind of thoughts), mindfulness (being fully present), and spontaneity.

We would likely be more relaxed, get more done, and learn more if we set time aside for awhile to reflect and be at peace. We are flooded by visual, auditory, physical clamor, and the demands of others. We need a place to retreat, to renew our strength. We don't necessarily have to go to a different location. Setting time aside where we live can mean finding a closet or a corner in a room without television, telephone, computer, or other items to distract us. I had a friend who would lie in an empty bathroom tub to reflect.

My wife has a book, *Find a Quiet Corner* by Nancy O'Hara, that suggests creating such a place. There you can discover how to "soar on wings like eagles; . . . run and not grow weary, walk and not be faint." (Isa 40:31) But first you must rest.

Where is your "quiet corner"?

Musings

God's Promise

> Our Father, in heaven, hallowed be Your name;
> You are our shepherd; We lack nothing. Your kingdom come;
> Your will be done, on earth as it is in heaven.
> You make us lie down in green pastures.
> You lead us beside quiet waters.
> You refresh our soul. You give us today our daily bread.
> You guide us along right paths for Your name's sake.
> And forgive us our debts, as we also have forgiven our debtors.
> Even though we walk through the darkest valley,
> We will fear no evil, for You are with us; Your rod and your staff, they comfort us.
> And lead us not into temptation; but deliver us from the evil one.
> You prepare a table before us in the presence of our enemies;
> You anoint our heads with oil; our cup overflows.
> Surely goodness and love will follow us all the days of our life,
> and we shall dwell in the house of the Lord forever.
> (Ps 23; Matt 6:9a–13b)
>
> Sincerely,
> God

Touch

We live in a very busy world. I read a novel about a woman who fell through a time warp from today's world into twelfth-century Wales. In a conversation with her new twelfth-century companions, she told them about people in the twentieth century: "But people who live in that world don't realize what they've lost along the way."[61] "Everyone behaves as if they are completely alone, even when—or especially when—surrounded by a crowd."[62]

We attach value to using our time efficiently. Taking time to attend to the people around us can feel like a waste. Why bother? We may never see them again. The character in the novel said, "It's because we don't depend on each other anymore."[63]

---

61. Woodbury, *"Daughter of Time."* 204.
62. Ibid. 205.
63. Ibid. 205.

What a lonely life we live! Life can be like a yacht race, sailing past each other so we can to get to the finish line and receive a trophy.

I am always surprised, delighted, and informed by each person that I take time to be with, even if it is just for ten or fifteen minutes. Some of the most interesting are the "invisible" people. This includes those who don't stand out in the crowd as well as those most of us think are strange and make us uncomfortable.

It is unreasonable to think we can spend time with everyone we pass during the day. But what we can do is focus on the face-to-face encounters. We can take time to be kind to the retail clerk, janitor, bag boy, and waitress or waiter. That acknowledgement may only be a drop in the pond of life, but it can initiate loving waves in the world with people we will never know.

I was enthralled by the television series, *Touch*, about an autistic boy who feels the pain of others and communicates to his father through numbers. Each episode begins with individual scenarios of people in different parts of the world. The well-written and sensitive script shows how even the most unlikely acts of kindness can touch others in the most distant places. Paul says that we are all one, and no one is less than the other. If we could all practice "paying it forward," (the title of another beautiful movie), the world would change like we cannot imagine.

We can't save the world, but we can start a revolution of love and kindness, one by one!

The Great Leap

There is a relatively new theory that helps explain the disarray and disorder in our lives. Fractal theory uses a mathematical formula to demonstrate order in what may at first look like chaos. Take a tree, for example. When you look at the whole tree, especially without leaves, it looks like a disordered mass of branches and twigs going in all directions. Fractal theory explains that a tree starts out in a "Y", and each branch of the "Y" creates another "Y", and so on. So there is an order that is not so apparent.

Chaos theory is another theory along this same vein of thought. Its premise is that an initial action will produce varying results which cannot be predicted. It has also been called the "butterfly effect." A paper presented by Edward N. Lorenz, Sc. D. at the Massachusetts Institute of Technology in December, 1972 was entitled: *Predictability: Does the Flap of a Butterfly's*

Musings

Wings in Brazil set off a Tornado in Texas?[64] It seems absurd, and yet, this armchair quantum physicist sees simplistic messages in both of these theories.

There is a DVD called *Fractals* that goes into more detail that you can stream or rent from *Netflix*. I felt a sense of awe and wonder at the incredible power of the universe we live in as I watched this DVD.

I hope I haven't lost you. This seemingly heavy topic offers me more evidence of the Power that has designed a creation beyond our understanding. We spend a great deal of time trying to create order out of our chaotic lives. Sometimes we try to do just that and end up hitting a wall of frustration. What then? We can always take "a leap of faith," a quote often attributed to Søren Kiekegaard, the great theologian. We can believe that something greater than ourselves has knowledge of what we don't understand.

All experiences are lessons for growth. The ones we cannot make sense out of or feel are unfair are understood by the One that put it all in motion.

The next time something doesn't make sense to you, "take a leap of faith" that the omniscient, all knowing One has it taken care of. We are probably not ready to understand it anyway.

Falling Short

Jesus said that "we all sin and fall short of the glory of God." (Rom. 3:23) I have come to believe that a lot of what Jesus said has a deeper meaning than the literal Biblical statement.

In this example, he could be pointing out that we all are wounded by past experience and that we carry those wounds within us. Unless we look deep inside (often with professional help), those wounds will cause us to react to others' opinions, choices, and actions in negative ways.

We can also be quick to point the finger of blame. You may have noticed that when you point a finger on your hand, there are three fingers pointing back at you. Those three fingers can be a reminder to look within as to what's getting stirred up. Find the part you are playing in the conflict. Doesn't your hand look like a gun pointed at someone? Blame can be explosive.

When we want to change someone's beliefs and behavior, it is usually because an old wound of ours is being stirred up. We may be afraid of being hurt again or that our lack of confidence will be revealed. We feel

64. Lorenz, "Butterfly."

self-conscious as if we're in the spotlight and try to divert the attention by suggesting that the other person is wrong!

If we don't like something in someone else, it often relates to something in us that we don't like. We may think that if we can change the other person, we will feel safe and secure. It doesn't work. Our insecurity lies within. We can't move on until we deal with our own demons. Nothing the other person does changes that.

Although it's only human to try and hold on to familiar ground, we can find stability with new opinions, beliefs and choices. If we are stuck where we stand, we can become as "pillars of salt." (Gen 19:26)

The greatest gift we can give to ourselves and others comes when we are aware of our wounds and don't allow them to affect our relationships.

Deal of a Lifetime!

What is temptation? Is it an act that leads to an immoral or sinful consequence?

Giving in to certain temptations can mean betrayal of our values and commitments to ourselves. Perhaps you make a pledge to yourself to simplify your life, to learn to live in a more minimalist style. You may decide to drive your automobile, as the expression goes, "until the tires fall off." Or, you decide not to buy another shirt until you get rid of one or two that you already have.

Temptation comes when multiple forms of media show us automobiles, clothes, new technology or other gadgets, and we feel guilty passing up a great deal! A good marketer knows how to appeal to our fear of being without or not fitting in.

One could almost say it is the new psychotherapy. We go to counseling because we feel our lives are not working. We are depressed, dealing with anxiety, and want something to make us feel good about ourselves again. Is this not the promise of advertising? Buy this new car and people will watch you drive by. Then you will feel significant again. Dress like this model and the men or women can't keep their eyes off of you! You will be attractive and acceptable.

"This above all: to thine own self be true . . . . " These are the words of Polonius to his son Laertes in Shakespeare's *Hamlet*.[65] He was not suggesting that his son be self-serving, but that he be clear about his values and

---

65. Shakespeare, "Hamlet."

Musings

know that they will be tested. We all face this each day. So where do we get this clarity about values that truly matter? If we take time to stop and think, we often know. Consequences of our own actions and those of others from the past have taught us. There is also that ancient Book that describes a life of value, one of real importance.

You do not walk alone in the battle to be true to *thine* own self, or maybe we should say, "to thy divine self."

Roots

My dad was in WWII, the Korean War, worked on advanced degrees, and was a United Methodist minister. I was moved as a child, and later by my own choices, a total of twenty-seven times in my life. (They would send me to the store for a loaf of bread and when I got back, they had moved!) It was disruptive *and* it was an education. I learned to adapt. However, the thing I missed most was familiarity, lifelong friends, stability, and roots.

Jesus said, "But since they have no root, they last only a short time. When trouble or persecution comes because of the word, they quickly fall away." (Matt 13:21) Being grounded, which is defined as "having a secure feeling of being in touch with reality and personal feelings"[66] or having roots, "the basis for a feeling of belonging in a particular place," is essential for our survival and sanity.[67]

Moving so many times, I tethered my roots to my grandmother's farm in southwest Virginia. It was the one place I could return to that I counted on for familiarity and belonging.

And yet, even those physical places we call home with their warmth, familiarity, and security don't always last. Thee farm house burned to the ground in the late sixties and the property was eventually sold.

In a world that has a lot of turmoil and keeps changing, we must learn to grow other roots. I now find my solid ground in the places where I am fed and accepted as I am. Today I feel warmth and security from my church, my extended family and my birth family. We have our squabbles and disagreements, but love and acceptance lift us from pettiness, encouraging the depth of our roots.

We need to trust in something that is familiar, and we need a place where we can belong. Continuing with the story Jesus was telling, we must,

66. Microsoft Encarta, "grounded."
67. Microsoft Encarta, "roots."

like a seed, be planted in good ground so we can feel anchored and lead a healthy, productive life.

Timeout

When I was a child and did something I was told not to do, I was put in timeout. It usually meant sitting in a chair staring at a corner. Time didn't go anywhere. I guess it was brief suspension from play.

I love to take things apart to see how they work, even words. Timeout doesn't mean that time ceases. It just means a change in how one spends time. It is a break or a rest. In sports, timeout means the game stops for a brief period.

Timeout from normal activities is necessary for our health. My timeout involves sitting on the porch watching nature, taking a nap, meditating or anything that allows me to stop doing and "just be".

How long has it been since you lay in the grass and spent time looking at the clouds? You say, "Oh, that is something children do!" Do you remember something about being childlike to experience heaven? (Matt18:3) My mind wanders to those days on my grandmother's farm lying on the hill above her house, watching a spiritual being make animals out of the clouds. I could even see stories being told by those clouds. The cool grass under my back and the delicate breezes caressing my body and soul felt like heaven to me. And no one was telling me what to do.

In a society that puts great value on producing results and frowns on cloud-gazing, be a rebel. Go find a grassy spot and watch the wonders of the heavens. They are there both day and night!

Circadian Muddle

When I come home from traveling a great distance, my mind feels like it's somewhere between where I've just been, and where I am now. I find that it takes me a couple of days to make the transition back to familiar routine and feeling grounded. Since I'm back from just such a trip, I write this brief musing until my mind comes home!

When you find yourself in transition, treat yourself gently. Go slowly. Don't rush into things. Become reacquainted with your surroundings. Embrace the familiar.

Musings

Abbie, our Shih Tzu, shows us how it is done. She comes into the house, walks around, sniffs, and checks out things to see that the familiar is still in its place. She finds her blanket, scruffs it up with her paws until it is just right, and lies down to let her body feel the comfort of being back home.

Think I will go and scruff up my blanket!

Missed Gifts

As I write this muse, my attention is suddenly drawn to movement out the window. I look closely to see a red-headed woodpecker on the side of a tree. What a beauty of creation with its fiery red feathers, its ability to cling to the side of a tree, and the rapid rat-a-tat-tat as it drills holes looking for insects.

These times for me are messages from our Creator to slow down and look more closely at the incredible beauty that surrounds us. Jesus spent his brief ministry using the simple and beautiful elements of life to teach about living abundantly. He pointed to fig trees, a poor widow giving her pennies to the church, flowers of the field, green pastures, still waters, and one lost sheep out of a herd. He stopped in the middle of work to talk and listen to a child, and much more.

I spent the last three weeks looking at the amazing beauty of the ocean, the intricacy and artistry of sea shells, awe-inspiring sunrises, and butterflies in an enclosure. There was also a very moving outdoor drama.

Yet, we don't have to go on vacation to see the beauty of this earth. Vacations give us the opportunity to get away from the routine of everyday life so that we have time to see beauty that we often miss. The dictionary describes routine as "something that is unvarying or boringly repetitive."[68] In horse and wagon times, horses had leather flaps on either side of their eyes so that they would focus on the road ahead, and not be distracted by anything but pulling the wagon.

I have also found that our anticipation and vision of retirement doesn't necessarily mean we aren't still hooked up to a wagon. It may just be a different wagon.

Our Creator has given us simple gifts. Unhook your wagon and sit awhile by the roadside.

A beautiful old song speaks to this:

---

68. Microsoft Encarta, "routine."

"'Tis the gift to be simple, 'tis the gift to be free.
'Tis the gift to come down where we ought to be.
And when we find ourselves in the place just right,
'Twill be in the valley of love and delight."[69]

The Good Ending

As I read or watch television and movies, I often take a moment to process what I have just experienced. I can be so caught up in the story that I may not fully realize the intense violence that has taken place. Are we drawn to extremes of actions and language for entertainment?

I am not advocating a governing body to limit freedom of speech. Censorship decisions remain each individual's responsibility. Yet, one wonders what will be "exposed" five, ten years from now! Even the radio is pushing the limits of FCC regulations. We have coined the term "shock jocks." What does that suggest to you? My grandmother's wisdom makes a lot of sense: "Trash in, trash out."

Is our violence-filled entertainment influencing the number of public shootings in this country? Repetitive exposure to violence often leads to it becoming a way of life. Look at countries where children have known nothing but war. We see those children carrying guns when they are barely big enough to lift them!

We can see films and read books that portray struggles between good and evil without intense violence. Many have a good ending. The Bible is full of violence and struggle; however, its message is to beat the "swords into plowshares" (Isa 2:4), and for the "lion to lie down with the goat." (Isa: 11:6) I like the promise of a good ending.

Releasing Spirits

Some of us look at the material things of life and only see things as they are. We look at a wooden box and see a container. We look at a cooked meal and see vegetables, meat, salad, and pie. We look at a painting and see a picture. How did these things get to be what we see?

You may know the story of Michelangelo working intently on a block of marble. The Pope came by and asked him why he was working so

---

69. Bracket, "Simple Gifts."

furiously. Michelangelo said, "I saw an angel in the marble and carved to set him free."[70]

We have been given all the materials we need to survive and create things that give us joy. We have been told that we are made in the image of the Creator; this suggests to me that we too are creators.

At times I am in awe at what we have created: houses, skyscrapers, automobiles, computers, tools, clothes, and meals. What if we looked at more than the results of our creations? What if we took time to look at the gifts of the raw materials and see what we have released?

The artist has taken mud and brought to life a beautiful sculpture. The woodworker has released a chest of drawers to hold our clothes from a tree. A seamstress uses wool from sheep or webs from a silkworm to create a dress or pants. The cook has taken carrots, potatoes, celery, and brought forth gifts from the earth to sustain us.

If we take time to look at the materials we are working with, we are all artists releasing spirits that have been there all along. We will have a greater respect for ourselves and for the gifts of the earth.

What spirits are you going to free today?

Heartfelt

Living in our heads is the farthest we can get from the ground. It is the place where all the chatter resides—the "shoulda," "woulda," "coulda" conditioning of our lives. When we follow these admonitions and deny our feelings, we often crash and burn.

We all have access to what's inside our heart but are often reluctant to share what we are feeling. Sometimes we are afraid that if we share our feelings, we will be guilt-ridden, ridiculed, or shamed. Yet, we have to discern who will be open to the truth of how we feel. Christ warned, "I am sending you out like sheep among wolves. Therefore, be as shrewd as snakes and as innocent as doves." (Matt 10:16)

We have focused on being as "shrewd as snakes" as a way of life, as evidenced by the rise in the number of ulcers, strokes, and heart attacks. Is much of this the result of stress and repressed feelings? "Heart attack" suggests that the heart is being attacked. If we aren't aware of our feelings and don't find a responsible way to express them, they may begin to attack us.

---

70. Michelangelo, Italian Artist, 1475 to 1564.

Don't we use the word "heart" to describe what is at the center of our feelings? This is also found in the book of ages, "You are the ones who justify yourselves in the eyes of others, but God knows your hearts." (Luke 16:15)

Go to that place where you truly live. Know your "heart." Be at peace about who you are.

A Time to Release

Most of us have objects of sentimental value around our homes. They are connected to someone dear to us or are valued because of a significant experience or milestone in our lives. We occasionally tell their stories to people. They are more than just lifeless objects. It is as if they have a spirit of their own. Yet, for the most part, they sit on a shelf or are hidden away in a drawer or closet.

If they could speak, oh, the stories they could tell. Wouldn't you like to know where they have been and what they have seen? However, we may want to release them after a long while collecting dust. Sometimes we find them a new home where they can continue to give of their spirit to others.

I had a collection of thirty-five stuffed teddy bears from different parts of the world, a lot of them handmade. One day I looked around. They were all staring at me and seemed to be saying, "Well?" (No, I had not lost my mind.) So I looked for places where they could give joy and began to release them, mostly to children who could love the fur off of them like in *The Velveteen Rabbit*.

Yesterday, I released a very special object, my father's communion kit that he carried through WWII and the Korean War. I often picture him carrying that kit from one ship to another in the boatswain's chair. This involved two men adjusting a rope-pulley system so the person in the chair could be safely transferred between the two ships moving in the waves. He had the harrowing experience of being "dipped" once or twice.

Dad gave the communion kit to me when I was ordained into the ministry, passing to me the tradition of serving communion. I often wondered, as I looked at that little black box, how many men had he united with the body and blood of Christ before they risked death in war? The communion of spirits through the contents of that simple black box offered courage and hope.

I found a beautiful new home for the communion kit. Our church has twenty-seven retired Chaplains who offer in-home ministry. Communion is a regular part of those visits. I was comforted that the communion kit would continue to give others peace and assurance of our connection to each other and to God. After years on my shelf, it was time for the communion kit to move on.

You will know when it is time to release a cherished item so it can continue to give the beauty of its spirit to others.

I still have the memories and stories from my Dad. They will always be a part of me.

The Benefits of Taking Time

We need to have quiet spaces between our doing. When working with power saws, we need to focus and take slow actions. Building something can turn out sloppy if we hurry. Driving a vehicle at a reasonable speed is crucial. An officer once said to me, "You are driving a two thousand pound bullet down the road." (That time it was a warning and I haven't had to be warned again!)

Do we use our time wisely in conversation? Often there is too little respect for the one talking. We allow many factors to block us—our mind's chatter, preconceived notions and prejudice, as well as the arrogance of thinking we have better information. Most of the time, we are preparing our rebuttal and not actually hearing or taking in what the other person is saying. When we aren't totally focused on the whole person who is speaking, we only get part of the message. Only empty words reach our ear drums.

Jesus said, "He who has ears, let him hear." (Mark 4:9) He was talking about more than vibrating skin stretched over cartilage. He was challenging the people (and his disciples) with an example from their daily life as a metaphor for living.

We need to hear more than the words a person is speaking. Why even talk if we are not trying to offer to others what we feel, how we believe, and what is important to us? When we respond too quickly, we do not allow what is said to sink in or hear the message behind the words. How often have we missed pleas for help from someone who is hurting, but doesn't say it directly? When we take time to listen, we receive the gift of connecting with another person's soul. Let there be spaces in our speech. We show genuine interest and respect when we allow a person to finish sharing their thoughts and feelings.

We need to think before we speak or we may miss crucial messages for help as well as messages that are meaningful in our lives. Besides if we speak too soon, we can end up chewing on our foot.

Choice

> "Freedom is the right to choose:
> the right to create for oneself the alternatives of choice.
> Without the possibility of choice, and the exercise of choice
> a man is not a man but a member, an instrument, a thing."[71]

Choice is the gift of freedom, and yet it includes the burden of responsibility. Not choosing is a gamble, because you must take what you get. If choices are made for us, we lose independence and give away our power.

Our lives are shaped by our choices. To choose is to live fully, boldly, and step out with faith. We can choose wisely, based on past outcomes, potential consequences, good research, moral strength, and spiritual guidance.

Choice involves risk and yet, if we remain neutral, indecisive, or waiting for certainty of outcome, we can be stuck, frozen, in suspension, and not living. There is no certainty as to the results of our choices. If we make a choice that doesn't have a good result, we can learn from it and make a different choice the next time around.

Choice is God's gift of trust in us.

Crisis and Thrill Junkies

Are we bored with life? Have we become so conditioned to the sensational that ordinary life seems dull? Live television shows or rock concerts have more and more lights, smoke, drum rolls, and fireworks. The more outrageous, skimpy, and suggestive the outfits are, the higher the ratings. Lady GaGa is a marketing genius when it comes being risqué and sensational.

Teens and young adults attempt to defy the laws of gravity in the X-Games. They are not only keeping up the orthopedic specialists, they have spawned a whole industry, sports medicine.

---

71. Macleish. American Poet and Writer, 1892 to 1982.

Musings

Is this adrenalin-pumping activity an addiction? Do we have a need for a constant high? Are we conscious of what it is costing us? Mundane activities easily bore many of us. If we aren't getting entertainment and sports stimulation, we may unknowingly create crises in our lives to fill the hole. Some people are so addicted to stimulation that if they don't have a problem to solve, they get anxious. So they create a crisis. It sounds sort of backwards doesn't it?

What is the cure? Like conquering all addictions, we have to create a program of withdrawal and a different way of experiencing the world. It is not easy. Being a bit of a stimulus junkie myself, I have learned that I pay a costly price when I absorb too much or push myself beyond my physical limits.

We first have to get reacquainted with our bodies. Our bodies speak! You have heard the saying, "I can feel it in my gut." If we take time to listen, we know when we are pushing its limits and when it is time to retreat. It is time to say "*no*" to what we and others expect of us.

Choosing wisely is a gift we can give ourselves. But sometimes we have to rely on a power greater than ourselves to avoid pushing ourselves over the line. After all, we have been told that our bodies are the temple of the Holy Spirit and we are to care for them.

Truth

Truth is integrated with culture. It is relative to a particular group of people and what they believe. It is often a bias developed by how we are taught and have been influenced.

Does what we believe become the truth? How do we believe?

- Seeing is believing . . . "If you hadn't shown me, I wouldn't have believed it!"
- Hearing is believing . . . "I believe it, because the news reporter said so."
- Saying is believing . . . "I believe they are wrong."
- Reading is believing . . . "Well, it says it right here in print."
- Counting is believing . . . "Count the change, if you don't believe me."
- Deducing is believing . . . "When you remove all else, what you have is the truth."
- Feeling is believing . . . "I feel certain that they will arrive on time."

We have used these statements to describe what we believe but does it make them true? How do we really distinguish the truth from beliefs? The dictionary defines truth as "conformity to fact or reality,"[72] and reality as "something that actually exists"[73]. This definition still leaves truth subject to opinion.

The world is changing so fast, it makes our heads swim. The computer you just bought is probably going to be obsolete within a short time. We seek stability. We all have a deep desire for something solid to stand on, not things that will slip through our fingers like sand. I remember hearing my Dad sing with great conviction and gusto, "On Christ the solid rock I stand, all other ground is sinking sand."[74]

When I am in doubt, frustrated with trying to keep up, being pummeled by unending opinions, or by people who claim, "It's God's honest truth," I climb upon that Rock for the quiet and certain peace it provides.

I do a lot of climbing, because I keep falling off. But truth is always there when I seek it!

Detours

I love this statement a friend sent me, "A truly happy person is one who can enjoy the scenery on a detour."[75]

We make plans, and they often don't come close to what we had envisioned. Life is full of shocks and surprises that seem to come out of thin air, knocking us flat on our backs. It's easy to get caught up in frustration and disappointment.

We have a limited amount of time here and, often as we get older, we have less energy. Those who spend their time in the land of grief, regret, and negativity never see the absurdity of human behavior and the humor it can bring with it. They miss what can be seen in the inevitable detours. Not only that, they often have physical evidence of living with negative reactions to failed plans. They are usually more wrinkled and shrivel up sooner than need be. They may have a perpetual look of just having eaten something nasty. I guess that is where the term "sour puss" came from.

---

72. Dictionary.com, "truth."
73. Dictionary.com, "reality."
74. Mote, American Pastor and Hymn Writer, 1797 to 1874.
75. Author Unknown

Musings

Detours from our intended directions give us experiences we would not have chosen. I remember driving from England to Scotland. Our destination was Edinburgh. We saw a small hand-painted sign at the beginning of a dirt road off to the right that said "pottery for sale". On a whim we took the detour. We met an Englishman who lived by himself in the country. He was delighted to have visitors. He plied us with stories and was proud to show us his workshop. We purchased a beautiful piece of pottery. As we were leaving, he waved and said, "Cheerio, " a term for "good bye". The spirit of this man also said to me, "Be of good cheer." The scenery was beautiful, and the experience was spiritual and uplifting.

The last lines of Robert Frost's poem, "The Road Less Traveled" say it best:

> "I shall be telling this with a sigh
> Somewhere ages and ages hence:
> Two roads diverged in a wood,
> and I—I took the one less traveled by,
> And that has made all the difference."[76]

Don't focus on the disappointment and frustration of detours. Enjoy the journey. It can hold unexpected treasure.

"If Only"

"If only" may be two of the most wasted words in the English language. It serves no purpose to say "if only". Our journey in life can only be walked in one direction. We can "if only" all day long, and it isn't going to change what has happened. These words bring up feelings of agony, despair, struggle, defeat, sadness, and frustration. Talking about ill-spent energy!

The old saying, "Don't cry over spilt milk" speaks to this. For example, you're talking and gesturing excitedly about what you are saying. There is a glass of milk or whatever beverage nearby, and you hit it with your waving arms. It hits the floor, breaks into a thousand pieces, and milk splatters everywhere. Most of us would stand there expressing our frustration and embarrassment by saying things like, "What an idiot I was. I should be more careful. Why did I put that glass there? Now, look what I have done. *If only* I

---

76. Lathem, "Frost", 105.

had not placed the glass there." Grousing isn't going to make that glass come back together, soak up the spilt liquid, and hop back up on the table.

A few people might say things like "Wow, what a fantastic mess! Look at the design the milk has made. It actually looks like a cow, or maybe a moose." Making these statements is certainly more fun than the "if only's" even though they don't change the consequences of our action. The words "if only" can offer a positive influence if they lead us to contemplate what we could have done differently. I think the wise prophet from old was telling us to stop saying "if only" when he said, "Who of you by worrying can add a single hour to your life?" (Luke 25:12)

Find creative thoughts and statements about the messes you make. Besides, it gives those around you something to talk about, seeing you talking to your mess!

The Jesus I Never Knew[77]

We are asked to believe the teachings of a man from the Middle East two thousand years ago. This is someone I never met face to face. We never had a two-way conversation. I had also never seen him in a photo or DVD. On one hand, it is amazing that intelligent and rational people have accepted his teachings. And yet, I'll have to admit, my life has been dramatically influenced by this mysterious person.

I had an email relationship with a spiritual brother whom I never met, never had a conversation with, and never saw a picture of until after his death. Here is an experience with a person of my time who influenced me greatly. The only connection was words. He never failed to respond to my email musings. We shared similar views and were mutually supportive.

This experience has reminded me that when I am feeling skeptical and so far removed from that person of two thousand years ago, I don't need physical proof of his presence. The universe keeps reminding me of a love that transcends time and physical presence.

I read a story that happened many years ago about a man who regularly visited a mental patient in a hospital. The patient never spoke. The staff would tell the man that he was wasting his time. However, he continued to come, sit, and tell the man stories about life outside. He would leave him an orange each time he visited. The man died and someone told the visitor

---

77. Yancy, "Book title."

that he spoke his first words in years. He said, "He (the visitor) was the only Jesus I ever knew."

We all have the living Christ in us. We must find a way to manifest this Christ spirit in us at each moment, and with each person, no matter what we have heard about them or think about them. We will be remembered and make a difference in the world. These actions transcend all religions and races. We often let fear keep us from bringing out the spirit.

To create a spiritual connection, one that goes beyond our speaking to, seeing, and hearing someone, is to be the Jesus I never knew.

Have you been the only Jesus someone knew?

Larger than Life

When I look at the ocean, I am struck by its immense presence, knowing that what I see represents only a small fraction of its existence. I am aware, and always amazed at the consistency of its movement. From the beginning of time, waves have broken against the shorelines, the same waves during the exodus of the Israelites from Egypt, during the time of Jesus, during the Crusades, during the building of our colonies, etc. Looking at the ocean and seeing the curvature of the earth on the horizon reminds me of how small we are. It was, is, and will always be there, with the waves moving in and out.

Each time I see the ocean from land's edge, I am awed. It is larger than life itself. The anticipation and excitement is the same as when I was a child. As we got closer to the ocean on family vacations, my sisters and I would stretch our necks across the front seat to yell out, "I see it first!" It was always a new and exhilarating experience even though we came back every year.

When I am at the ocean, the everydayness of life seems to disappear, and I feel like I'm standing on sacred ground. Maybe the presence of this vast body of water represents more than the survival of a water-dependent planet. Could it be a reminder of an ever larger Presence, one we only see glimpses of, one that has been here before and since life began, one that is constantly alive and moving? The ocean draws our attention in a way that touches our souls.

Each of us must look within to see what we feel in the face of an enormous phenomenon. After all, it is created by something larger than itself.

"May the Force be with You"[78]

Let's imagine coming upon a muddy creek as we are walking through the woods. A rope hangs about waist high. It looks like it is long enough to swing us over. If you grab the rope, swing to the other side, and let go when just your toes touch the ground, your body will be at an angle and you'll fall back into the muddy creek.

How do you get across without falling back into the mud? The only way, as we used to say as children, is to get a "runny go." Grab the rope, swing high to the other side until the rope reaches its highest arc, and let go when your body is moving forward. Your momentum will carry you to solid ground.

As a child, I remember being a rope swinger. Most often I was swinging off a bank into a pond or lake. It took confidence to let go of the rope in mid-air. I saw some of my friends who were fearful of letting go of the rope dragged back to the bank through the dirt and bushes.

Momentum is the force of forward movement. In the movie *Star Wars*, the characters representing the good forces of life often said, "The Force be with you." Luke Skywalker, with the help of Yoda, was able to use the force for noble causes. Luke had the struggle of letting go and trusting the force on several occasions.

We have access to such a force in life. We were born with that force within us. As we grow and become aware, we can feel that force within and around us. We have the freedom to trust it and use the force for spreading positive energy into the world. Or we can give into dark forces of fear that drag us back in the mud. We can take. We can use up. We can leave a trail of destruction behind us. If we live self-centered lives, we not only suck the life out of all around us, we also begin to shrivel within. Dark acts and feelings drain our souls.

What a powerful life we have been given! We can tentatively grab the rope, hold on with fear until the tip of our toes touch ground, only to find ourselves falling back in the muck and mire. Or, we can grab that rope with gusto, fly through the air with confidence to the rope's highest arc and let go, landing on our feet!

---

78. *Star Wars*, Movie.

Musings

Prayer

Those of us who believe in a Higher Power often pray every day. Prayer isn't necessarily a formal, get on your knees kind of prayer. (A lot of us would be in trouble if getting on our knees were a requirement for prayer!) I believe prayer is as simple as hoping or wishing positive thoughts for someone who is hurting or needs help. We're told we don't even have to say it to our Higher Power; "your Father knows what you need before you ask him." (Matt 6:8)

A prayerful attitude is a way of life. It includes being conscious of caring for others, based on knowing we don't navigate this journey alone.

There is one verse of prayer in the Bible that has always puzzled me. In Matthew, we are told, "Ask and it will be given to you; seek you will find; knock and the door will be opened." (Matt 7:7) How many of us have pleaded fervently and constantly for God to remove some barrier or take away our pain or illness? We wait and we still suffer. We feel our prayers aren't answered. Do we expect to get an answer the way we want or envision it?

Prayer works, but the result is probably going to be different than we imagine. Maybe the answer is receiving the strength to live with our condition. That doesn't mean we're supposed to flaunt our pain or live like we're victims of it.

Humility means we avoid drawing attention to ourselves. We can be humble and still seek the strength of others in the challenges of life. I want a lot of people praying for me. Let's not let our expectation of the results of prayer cause us despair, or feel like God hasn't answered us.

I like the expression, "That which doesn't kill us will make us stronger." Have you not met people who have lived most of their life with pain or physical limitations, and yet they still have a zest and love for life? And we ask, how can they be so full of life when they have to live with their health issues?

We have probably heard the quote, "I cried because I had no shoes until I met a man who had no feet."[79]

All of this rambling is not to make us feel guilty, but to put into perspective the bumps, falls, and being knocked silly that we encounter as we walk the walk. Someone hears us.

---

79. Anonymous

Against The Tide

What is the motivation behind your goals? A lot of us choose based on what others expect or would think of us. We fear going against the pressure to fit in. If our goal is to be liked and fit in, even after we think we have been accepted, we often find ourselves disappointed. These are goals based on ego and fear, not the spirit within us.

A goal of getting married because everyone else our age is doing so is a recipe for disaster. The goal to take a job primarily because the money is good likely will lead to regret, boredom, and misery. If we aim to please someone despite conflicts with our values, we will feel resentment.

There is a lot of pressure in the world pushing us in directions that are not of our choosing. Goals must come from the core of who we know we are. It takes a strong person to stand up against forces that are trying to control us or put us in the box others envision for us. Look before you leap. Take time to observe your feelings, your needs, and what fits for you. Be real about the consequences and benefits. This is not a suggestion to be totally self-serving, but to know what is in your heart.

Our country is founded on goals that were different than those of the monarchy we came from. That is why we call July 4th Independence Day, i.e., the day we celebrate freedom from being controlled by another person or society.

I love body surfing in the ocean. Reaching the goal of a good ride is to go against the tide. I have to force my body through crashing wave after wave until I get to the place where the waves are just beginning to break, to allow them to carry me back to the beach.

Much of the time life is like that. We have to go against the forces until we get to the place where we can find the wave that suits us, and ride in with a sense of joy and success.

Find your wave and enjoy the ride.

"Barn Raisin'"

We are community creatures. We were not created to live alone and totally depend on ourselves. Being in community gives our lives more balance. I have always loved the Amish way of living. When someone can't plow their field because of illness, the neighbors come and do it for them. If a barn needs to be built, the community makes a celebration with everyone involved. This country was built on this "barn-raising" spirit.

I grew up as somewhat of a loner. I have two younger sisters. Being the oldest with no brothers, a lot was expected of me. Being a minister's son put me in a class by itself. In order to survive, I became pretty self-sufficient. I had in my mind the way things should go, and I felt I was the only one who could do it right. Although I admired the community spirit of the Amish and other close-knit communities, I still resisted being part of a team. Moving often didn't encourage our family in becoming an integral part of a community.

I started learning late in life that it is often much more fun and efficient to work side by side with others. Not only did the job get done faster, but I learned new and different ways to do things when I had thought there was only one way.

Sitting together and sharing the stories of our lives brings a unique sense of comfort, security, and completeness. This sense of communion, a relationship of emotional and spiritual closeness, helps us through loss, illness, and tragedy. It also makes sacred the celebrations of life. During those times we truly know we are not alone. There are others who feel and experience what we encounter in life's journey.

This kind of community spirit is making a comeback. There are groups forming to grow crops for the poor. There are many support groups available so that we don't have to feel alone in specific needs.

Gather some people, find someone who needs their "field plowed" or "barn raised," and celebrate the joy of communion of the spirit. I have such a group. We meet every Wednesday morning. I have no doubt that if I needed something, all I would have to do is call. Thanks, guys!

Tiredness to Tenacity

Even when you feel you have given all you can, or you wake up and don't have the energy to lift your feet, you have to move anyway. Where do you go to find the "the getup and go when it's done got up and went?"

Of course, our bodies are telling us that there are times we must stop and rest. Most of us push ourselves beyond reason. Then there are those days when discouragement, depression, or despair drags us down. You know those times when your body feels like lead, when you just want to crawl back in bed and pull the covers over your head. You don't feel you have an ounce of energy left.

We have reserves. We are usually not aware of them. They are there, down deep within. We have seen people with this kind of resolve portrayed in movies, read about them in the papers, and seen them first hand. And we shake our heads and wonder how in the world they keep on when all odds seem to be against them.

During the 1996 Paralympics, I was a volunteer. I saw Tony Volpentest, with no feet or hands, win the one hundred meter dash in 11.36 seconds. He had two prosthesis—like ski tips. That is only 1.5 seconds slower than Donovan Bailey ran it with legs and feet in the Olympics of that same year! I saw a high jumper with one leg jump over six feet. These and many others at this event astounded and humbled me.

There was a homeless girl who fought against all odds. She hadn't finished high school. She was alone. She decided to get her GED. She studied in apartment buildings where she slept, sometimes under the stairwell. She succeeded with high grades. Making a long story short, against overwhelming odds, she graduated from Harvard.

In counseling I saw people who came from a horrible, abusive childhood being able to turn that nightmare around, counseling young people in similar situations or just leading a normal life without resentment and anger.

Where does this extra determination come from? Maybe it comes from being stubborn enough not to let life get you down, going from limitation to tenacity. Sitting and thinking about how bad we feel doesn't make those feelings disappear. Sometimes just getting up and getting involved opens the door to those reserves that we all have.

Balance

I'd like to add "balance" to the two previous musings: "Tiredness to Tenacity," and "Against the Tide." "Against the Tide" was about pushing against and through the forces that go against us in life. "Tiredness to Tenacity" encourages us to not let our limitations defeat us or keep us from being productive.

When should we use good sense and act on what our bodies are telling us? Remind yourself that you're living in a culture that says things like "get ahead regardless of the cost", "a rolling stone gathers no moss," and, "don't just sit there, do something."

We all need balance between exertion and rest. There is a difference between choosing to let the body and mind rest, and ignoring reason to reach some goal. Reaching a goal is a journey not unlike taking a hike through the woods. An enriching and productive hike is one where we stop periodically to look at something unusual or beautiful. We also need to stop, drink water, rest, and eat a granola bar from time to time. We have to judge for ourselves a reasonable distance to hike based on our physical abilities.

As I age, I am experiencing limitations that are reasonable for my age, and yet, because of society's focus on success and getting ahead, I struggle with guilt and frustration about not being able to do what I once did. A twenty or thirty year-old mindset can be dangerous in a sixty or seventy year-old body!

I'm not sure anyone ever told me what I was trying to get ahead of! We all want to feel productive and needed. But we need creativity in deciding what we are able to do. You may have to give up running ten kilometer road races, and instead, ride a bicycle, walk or swim each day.

I used to run a ten kilometer (6.2 miles) in forty-two minutes. Now my knees won't let me. So I walk every day. I used to enjoy an evening glass of wine with crackers and cheese. Now my stomach won't let me, instead I have a glass of Metamucil and two prunes!

Hey, prunes are pretty good!

Stories

Our lives are made up of the stories we have experienced and allowed to define who we are. In most cases our parents or caretakers taught us things about life that they felt would protect us or benefit us as we transverse the challenges ahead of us.

These were stories they were taught or learned in the trial and error living that they passed on to us. I am not just talking about lengthy narrative stories with characters, although we all heard these growing up. I am talking about rules, warnings, and threats if we engaged in certain behaviors. We were all told, "Don't talk to strangers." It may have served us as children, but if we still believed them, we'd be living in isolation. The one that didn't make sense to me was, "Always wear clean underwear. You never know when you might be in an accident." Well! If you are in an accident, you might as well forget about clean underwear!

As a child we needed to know about consequences, and how to set limits. However, some of these "stories" left wounds that we still carry with us, affecting how we act and relate to others. They can cause blocks to healthy relating with others, even damage in our relationships.

In my practice, it seemed that the most damaging stories were about sex. Much of the advice given left lasting wounds as well as feelings of guilt, fear, and shame. Our sensuality is a gift from the Creator. However, many received negative information about their sexuality.

How do we keep the stories that wounded us from continuing to control our lives and harm our relationships?

First, we can accept that those stories were our parents' stories. As we heard them, we incorporated them into our being. But now we can realize that they are just stories and not who we are now. We can look at them and decide if they are getting in the way of who we really are and the gifts we have to offer.

To allow such stories to rule us is to be stuck in childhood or adolescence. The mature adult can soothe the wounded child within and can reconnect that child with its innocence.

We are not our stories. We are loving beings. I believe that when Jesus said not to hide our light under a bushel, that bushel represented all the stories we carry around that hide the core of our beautiful being. We are beings of light and have the power to release that light to shine!

Smiles or Tears

We can spend a good bit of time bemoaning situations that didn't turn out the way we wanted them to or being sad because something we enjoyed has ended. I find myself doing this with a good book by wishing it would continue or agonizing over the outcome. All good experiences as well as bad situations will end. But the reality is they will be replaced with new ones. If we spend more time enjoying or learning from our journey rather than focusing on what we didn't like, we will be richer for it.

When you think about it, crying because life doesn't follow our plans is a waste of good energy and time. What's done is done. We know this. We have heard it many times, and yet, we often fall back into wishing for what once was.

Musings

Lot's wife was told not to look back. She didn't believe it, and look what happened to her? I often wondered why she was turned into a pillar of salt. But when I think about it, salt is used to preserve things. So perhaps she was preserved in a perpetual state of looking back!

This saying came to me in an email, "Don't cry because it is over. Smile because it happened."[80] Wow! I love that! I don't want to miss any of the joy of the journey, the experiences, and the lessons that I could learn. Even though it is difficult to smile about the tragic and painful encounters of life, they teach us lessons, and prepare us for the journey ahead. It just takes a while to process them. We must grieve for a bit first. Then comes a time to jump into the vehicle, look out the windows, and enjoy more stops along the way.

I wish you more smiles than tears for your journey.

Castles in the Air

You may have heard the term, "building castles in the air." We all build castles in the air. The problem comes when we try to live in them.

"A neurotic is a man who builds a castle in the air. A psychotic is the man who lives in it. A psychiatrist is the man who collects the rent."[81]

Life becomes problematic when we stay in our heads fantasizing about ideas or goals. In movies, television, or literature, we often see a character with big plans who isn't realistic about his ability to make them happen. We say about these people that they have their heads in the clouds.

There is nothing wrong with dreaming or visualizing. Both are part of having a creative or visionary mind. Henry David Thoreau said, "If you have built castles in the air, your work need not be lost; that is where they should be. Now put the foundations under them."[82]

Once you have built your castle in the air, come back to earth and do the hard work of making it real. Jesus said (paraphrasing), "If we build *castles in the air* they will most likely be blown away when the rains and storms come." (Matt 7:24–27)

So what are the materials to build solid foundations under our castles?

They come from one who used everyday stories to tell about a life that can withstand the tests and winds. The more I read about what Jesus said,

80. Wikiquote, Anonymous Quote.
81. Lawrence, American Playwright, 1915 to 2004.
82. Thoreau, "Walden."

the more I realize how well it fits together. It makes sense about how to navigate our journey.

Every day gather materials that will stand the test of time, and you will feel more secure in a world blown about by the winds and whims of those who are blowing the loudest. Success is about being grounded. Build your "castles in the air", and put a foundation under them in the here and now.

Caring versus Caring For

Taking care of our own needs before we take care of another person's needs is not being selfish. It is just being responsible. We may not be encouraged in this society to take care of our own needs. Praise is often given to those who sacrifice themselves for others.

Have you ever thought that when you try to solve someone's problems or do for them what they could do for themselves that you are dishonoring them? You are enabling them to be dependent. You may be taking away their sense of self-worth and pride in accomplishing tasks for themselves. This is not caring for them.

When I was in seminary, I had a part time job in a nursing home. One day I was in a patient's room when a nurse brought his meal to him. She set the tray on the table. She fit a spoon with a large piece of cork taped around the handle into his hand and told him to try and eat. The gentleman had rheumatoid arthritis. His fingers were bent sideways. He pleaded for her to feed him. She wouldn't. He scooped up a spoon full of peas and shakily tried to move them to his mouth, but proceeded to throw them over his head. The next spoonful of mashed potatoes went up his nose. It sounds funny, but it was very painful to watch. I thought she was being cruel. I challenged her behavior in the hall. She said that he had very little left that he could do by himself, and they were trying to teach him to feed himself to give him a sense of pride and accomplishment. And, after a few weeks he was feeding himself, smiling, and not complaining. She cared enough for him to help him regain some of his self-worth.

To respect other people's abilities to take care of themselves has sometimes been called "tough love."

We are compassionate people. We don't like to see people suffer. We think we are sharing our love by jumping in and taking over. If we hadn't allowed our infants to fall in their attempts to walk, they would never have learned to walk by themselves! We need to set aside our automatic reaction to rescue someone, and consider whether we are being helpful or harmful.

We have to ask ourselves, "Are we taking care of someone or caring for them?" Those who are ill or those physically or mentally challenged need taking care of, yet even they need for us to care enough to find ways for them to have personal successes, no matter how small.

When I Am Old and Feeble

When I am old and feeble and no longer seem to have fun
Take me out and place me in the sun
Where I can sit and reminisce about times gone by
And look to the heavens to watch birds fly

Don't yell or fuss or treat me like a child
Sit and discuss with me intellectual things for awhile
I may be wrinkled, can't see or hear too clearly
But your respect helps maintain my dignity

Don't leave me for long periods alone
Come visit me or call me on the phone
You may think me to be somewhat daft
But I have stories that can make you laugh

So after we have talked and I have been well fed
Go with me and help me to my bed
Know my circulation is not so good
So make sure you wrap my feet warmly if you would

I will drift off to sleep feeling content
Deeply grateful for the time that you have spent
We can both be assured of the God above
Who brought us together with a gift called love.

—Edward L. Boye, 2012

Musings

"Ya Hear Now?"

Those of us who live below the Mason-Dixon line have our own language. I was born in Virginia. That makes me a Southerner. I grew up with southern colloquialisms. There are old sayings like "out yonder". What does "yonder" mean? "Hits over yonder" was the way it was spoken. "I'm fixing to go over yonder." I don't know how the South adopted it. I haven't heard it in any other part of the country. Some would call it ignorant, but we know what we are talking about.

Then I came across a famous line in one of Shakespeare's plays: "But, soft! What light through yonder window breaks? It is the east and Juliet is the sun."

And I thought we Southerners owned the word! Not to worry, we have plenty of others. My mother used to say, "I am going to jerk a knot in your tail." I wasn't sure how she could do that. I didn't ask her because I knew what she meant! Another one was, "He was so ugly when he was born, the doctor slapped his momma." If someone said something or did something not too smart, we'd say, "He's one brick short of a load." And I heard one the other day that I had not come across, "He's crazier than a blind dog in a meat house." Think about that one for a minute.

So much is said in such few words. I love it! "I am as happy as pig in slop."

Exposed

There is a lot in the news lately about whether we can have privacy and also be secure in our country. Although there are different levels of what should be made public and what should remain in the realm of efforts to maintain our security, it is often not realistic to think we can have security and privacy at the same time. We haven't had privacy for ages. Someone is always sharing some information or a story about someone else. We call it gossip. And I really love the one where someone says, "He told me not to tell anyone, so I will tell you and you can't tell anyone else." That is supposed to make it ok?

We have widespread electronic surveillance in our lives . . . making credit checks, and watching what internet sites we visit so they can send us advertising. And our wireless cell phone conversations are picked up by others at times. Ask Prince Charles and Camilla about that one.

Musings

We are compassionate people and we are ready to help those in need. This makes us vulnerable to computer hackers who initiate pleas for help, imitating someone we know.

We just experienced this with an old email account that we are closing (not the one I am now using). The email said we were stranded in the Philippines because everything had been stolen, and included a plea to wire money so we could get back home. This experience can put us back in touch with humility, as opposed to being overconfident or naïve. We are sad if that our family and friends had an initial shock that we were in trouble before they had time to realize it was a scam. And this one has been around awhile.

How do we protect ourselves? We make ourselves aware of the types of scams that are used to fleece people. We find ways to check the legitimacy or, too often, the falsehood of these types of emails. Con artists have been around from the beginning of time. It is more prevalent in this age of technology. We were advised over two thousand years ago: "Behold, I send you out as sheep among wolves, be wise as serpents and innocent as doves." (Matt 10:16)

Thanks for all of those who called to check on us. It feels good to be loved by such an extended family!

Beauty or Beast

I was looking in the mirror the other morning and wondered why my hair line keeps moving back. Where was all this hair going? As I contemplated this, I noticed my ears. There were tufts of hair shooting out like porcupine quills. And my eye brows looked like grape arbors shading my eyes. I also noticed that certain parts of my body are sagging. When I look at the top of my legs, especially if the skin is pushed together some, it looks like the bottom of a dry creek bed. I was comforted knowing all of this is the result of being a human form of *The Velveteen Rabbit*. Remember most of his fur was rubbed off because he was so loved.

Beauty aids and surgical stretches, scrapes, and tucks are a multi-billion industry. We seemed to be obsessed with keeping our bodies as young as possible for as long as possible. Someone has even written a book titled, *Younger Next Year*. Is it an attempt to deny the reality of aging and death? Is it that we are so insecure that we rely on our looks and what we wear to make us feel good about ourselves? And some of these attempts at beauty have some pretty scary results. I have seen face lifts on women and men that looked like their pony tail was tightened by a steel vise, freezing them with "a perpetual look of surprise".

Doesn't it say somewhere that we shouldn't spend our time worrying about our clothes or being obsessed about our looks? "Therefore I tell you, do not worry about your life, what you will eat or drink; or about your body, what you will wear. Is not life more than food, and the body more than clothes?" (Matt: 6:25) This passage suggests that we spend more time on what is important—the real beauty of life—how we treat ourselves and others and taking time to see beyond the reflection that we are made in the likeness of the Creator. Since most people have not seen the Creator, we can take that to mean we are being encouraged to focus on deeper, more lasting concerns.

A mirror is only a reflection. A reflection occurs only on the surface. It takes more effort to look deeper and see the beauty within ourselves and others. Narcissus only saw his reflection and missed the beauty around him and at the bottom of the pond.

This doesn't mean we don't occasionally trim our eyebrows and ears, if only to see and hear better!

Now where are those scissors?

Perturbation

I was introduced to this word some years ago in a weekend intensive seminar. The word was used in a theory from the book, *The Critical Path*, by Buckminster Fuller, an American author, designer, inventor, and futurist. The word is perturbation.

Perturbation, in a nutshell, is when any system absorbs such an overload of energy that the system becomes unstable, and is then transformed. An example would be when water is brought to a boiling point and becomes steam.

From personal experience, we know that we are often perturbed by circumstances. Obstructions stand in the way of reaching our dreams and goals. If we accept that the path to change will involve perturbation, then we will eventually succeed and be changed. We need determination to keep going up against whatever is blocking our way until we break through. Our dreams, hope, and a good dose of tenacity provide the energy that will eventually dissolve what stands in our way.

Musings

It is through tough challenges that we grow. The pain comes with giving up old habits, and conditioned, automatic responses of word, thought, and action. When we accept that we are going to be perturbed at times, we are more likely to come out transformed on the other side.

I have always encouraged people to go to college, if at all possible. You don't come out of four years of reading, experiments, essays, and tests (perturbation) without seeing the world from a different perspective.

There are many opportunities to experience perturbation, so when it happens to you, don't give up. Know that you are in a process of transformation. I believe this is what Paul meant when he said, "Therefore, if anyone is in Christ, he is a new creation; the old has passed away, behold, the new has come." (2 Cor 5:17)

Beyond Greeting: Part I

I used to ride a motorcycle. When I first started riding, I noticed riders coming toward me on the other side of the road. They would take their left hand off the handlebar and extend their arm out toward the road. I soon learned that it was a signal of solidarity and bonding. It was like saying, "I got your back," or "We have to stick together because of the dangers of riding a motorcycle." It was a great feeling that complete strangers suddenly felt like brothers and sisters.

I also belonged to the Honda Motorcycle Club of America. One of the benefits was that you could call the main office if you had bike trouble or any need really, and they would get in touch with the closest member to come to you. Although there are all kinds of people riding motorcycles these days, even the road-worn, roughest person covered in tattoos would likely come to your aid.

This certainly speaks of a caring and supportive community. Our man of Galilee definitely knew no boundaries when it came to humanity. If called, would we race out to the aid of someone that we did not know? Are we afraid or too cautious? If more of us reached out without letting our prejudged labels keep us imprisoned in fear, likely it would send out waves of peace and acceptance to change our anger-torn world.

There is a deaf person that I see occasionally. When he sees me, he automatically points his two fingers to his eyes, and then points the two fingers to me. It is short hand sign language for "Good to see you", and in his eyes I see "You are my friend." That experience lifts my spirit every time it happens, because it transcends any human or mental limitation that can get in the way of our connecting to each other's souls.

These are the kinds of treasures I store in the barns of my heart, because nothing can destroy them.

Beyond Greeting: Part II

Occasionally, you will hear others say "Namaste" as a greeting or parting comment. It comes from the Sanskrit language and means "I bow to you." "It has a spiritual significance of negating or reducing one's ego in the presence of another. The real meeting between people is the meeting of their minds. When we greet another, we do so with Namaste which means "may our minds meet", indicated by the folded palms before the chest. The bowing down of the head adds a gracious form to this extension of friendship in love and humility."[83]

Most cultures have such rituals. I believe it is part of our programming. It is the acknowledgement of the universal need to not feel alone, to feel safe with mutual connection, to respect each other, and to even go beyond the physical contact and meeting of minds to a joining together of souls.

We have a ritual in this culture that we do routinely without giving it much thought—shaking hands upon meeting. It signifies the two coming together in greeting and welcome. I have heard that the practice came from showing another person that you had no weapon in your hand. In a way this still holds true. "I come to you as a friend with no intention of harm."

Touch is essential for survival in this world. Do we really think about the warmth and touching that is involved in a handshake? If our deeper intention is to say "I am humbled that you are willing to meet me with your touch," it sends a spiritual message of soul connection. It opens us to another person with feelings of love and respect. Think about it the next time you shake hands. Be aware of the deeper connection. It will be conveyed through your hand as well as your eyes and deep from within your soul.

Namaste.

---

83. Sanskrit Documents, "Namaste."

Musings

Bought and Paid For

When we hear or see the word "crown", we often think of a head piece made of gold and jewels. The type of crown I want to focus on is metaphorical, one not necessarily obtained by our own efforts. American Novelist, James Baldwin made this statement, "Your crown has been bought and paid for. All you have to do is put it on your head."[84] This is not just a religious statement made in reference to Jesus. Baldwin is suggesting that we open our eyes and recognize that many people have paid the price for us to be where we are today, some still living, most not.

Many cultures honor their ancestors, particularly Asian and American Indian cultures. With the exception of Memorial Day in the US, we don't often think about the price paid by those who have gone before us.

I think of what I have, what I know, and where I live—and how I wouldn't have most of it unless my ancestors paid the price. Some would say, "I worked hard all my life to get where I am. I deserve what I have paid for with blood, sweat, and tears." There is nothing wrong with effort and sacrifice, but I am humbled by knowing that what we have is largely built on the shoulders of those who have gone before us.

I still believe that those ancestors are in a place to guide us. We are not alone. So as we navigate the river of life, know that we also are paying a price so those who come after us can put on their crown.

Fame and Fortune

I am often surprised when I discover the humanity of a famous person. When we see them, we can easily assume that they are Teflon-coated, and larger than life. We would like to think if we had their money and fame, life would be easier for us.

If we were honest, most of us would like to tell people that we have met or even better, personally know someone who is famous. "Oh, yeah, I know Brad Pitt. I ran into him in New Orleans in a restaurant." Some of us over the years have gotten an autograph from someone well known or had our picture taken with them. Why?

Does it help us to cover up the fact that we don't value ourselves and our accomplishments because we don't make *People Magazine*? This earthly house is not built upon a foundation of fame and fortune. It rides steadily

---

84 SearchQuotes, "Baldwin."

on the shoulders of the salt of the earth—dedicated, giving, and loving folks like me and you. We are told to give in secret and to pray without drawing attention to ourselves to be rewarded. I think the reward starts in our sincerity of giving, acting, and praying from the heart. Some would say, "Wait. It also says "let your light shine before others so they may see your good deeds. . . . " (Matt 5:16) I don't think he is saying to light up a stadium and perform a concert. It is all about intention. What is our intention? Is it to be seen and heard, or to give quietly and love with sincerity? This is done all the time without front page headlines. (Although, wouldn't you prefer reading about small acts of kindness than the mostly negative sensationalism?)

For there are many who make a life focused on being seen and having their reward. Too often we hear about some actor or entertainer who is no longer popular committing suicide. How empty fame and fortune becomes at that moment.

Feel the blessing of being one of the common folk. Your gifts are solid, lasting, and, thank God, not empty fodder for the tabloids.

Plan B

In the first grade, we were served a full lunch with dessert. I always loved dessert, so my goal was to get through the main meal to have dessert. Several times a week we would have a mixture of white, brown, and yellow goop. It looked nasty, and wasn't what I looked forward to. I always gave it away to eager classmates, puzzled that they were so happy to get it. One day I decided to stick my finger in it for a taste. Wow, it looked bad but tasted wonderful. I discovered banana pudding!

We have dreams. We have goals. We plan ahead. We focus on what we want. We work hard to reach what we envision. We spend a great amount of energy getting there only to find out that our dream has evaded us, failed to work out or wasn't what we expected.

What then? Do we give up? Do we sit in defeat? Do we wallow in despair? Unfortunately, too many do just that—never tasting the beauty and well-being of success or feeling good about reaching a goal even though it has taken on a different image than we envisioned.

Wait! What about plan B? Someone once said, "I came that you may have life and have it abundantly!" (John 10:10 RSV) Could this mean that we have a second chance, another route to dreams, goals, plans, and desires?

Musings

When I think of abundance, I think of unlimited experiences and opportunities each day, each moment. The awareness of abundance is based on attitude. No matter what circumstances we face, we can see those circumstances as dragging us down or as challenges that give us strength, understanding, and multiple choices. Challenges are opportunities for optimism and may involve some risk. However, they don't keep us stuck. They tell us that there is always a Plan B. Sometimes Plan B is even better than we anticipated with Plan A.

A Profound Wisdom

Living in a competitive society often leads us to put a lot of pressure on ourselves. We feel we have to keep up with the rest of the world or we will be left behind, not fit in, or seem ignorant. This pressure causes a lot of worry, stress, and complaining which only heaps on more negativity to our state of being. It seems such a waste of energy, yet it's almost automatic—a natural reaction to the threat of misery.

It is human to be cautious and concerned about our actions and the results. The good news is we don't have to remain in these dark places or make a habit of them.

Some time ago I saw the movie *The Best Exotic Marigold Hotel*.[85] One line was repeated by Dev Patel in the role of Sonny Kapoor every time someone would complain or express a worry: "Everything will be alright in the end, and if it is not alright, it is not the end."

This declaration is one of those simple bits of wisdom that causes most of us to be awed or stopped in our tracks. It is such a simple statement and, yet, so profound. It is a beautiful way of expressing hope.

I smile every time I think about it. It speaks volumes. On one hand, if you are still alive, it is not the end so there is hope that our situation will change. On the other, everything will be alright if it is the end, especially when you have faith that the end promises hope for something beyond this life.

Remember when you are hurting: "Everything will be alright in the end, and if it is not alright now, it is not the end!"

---

85. Twentieth Century Fox, "Exotic."

Stories

We need to tell our stories, especially the stories that relate to pain and suffering. Keeping these experiences inside can often harden or build a protective barrier around our heart. It is interesting that we speak of hardening of the arteries from such things as our diet, lack of exercise and stress. We could also say that the work of keeping painful stories and experiences inside can be stressful and lead to physical consequences.

Dr. Dean Ornish, a cardiologist and Clinical Professor of Medicine at the University of California in San Francisco, directed a study with patients who had coronary heart disease (narrowing of the heart arteries that often leads to heart attack).[86] His study involved a group following a very low-fat diet with the addition of an exercise program. What was different about this program from others is that he also involved the group in telling their stories and learning to live more gently. Blood flow studies before and after the interventions showed the earliest evidence that heart artery narrowings could be reversed. It could be said that the heart began to open up.

I have often heard people say that their father wouldn't talk about his war experience. Most of these fathers sat on their emotions. Many were not available emotionally to their wives and children. Obviously there is pain in the telling, because it involves reliving a painful experience. Can we tell the stories again and be able to live through them? We most assuredly can in the safety of love and acceptance. Wouldn't an incredible burden be lifted in letting trusted others see inside? It is though the telling that we release the pain.

A client in my counseling practice came for his first visit visibly stiff with stress. He finally began to tell his story of his time of Vietnam. He spent the whole hour reliving those horrible experiences, and finally at the end of the hour, his body just slumped into the couch. A burden was lifted. When he arose to leave, there was an imprint of sweat on the couch where he sat, visible evidence of his letting go.

Love is the salve that softens the hardened heart.

---

86. Ornish, "heart."

Musings

"Set-R-Down"

Too often we let situations bother us. If we have done something that turns out to be a mess or failure, we go over and over it in our minds. We wish we could go back and do it differently. It becomes a constant nagging thought.

We come across someone who believes differently than we do. It makes us uncomfortable, so we spend time and effort trying to convince them to see it our way. A lot of energy can be involved. We even lose sleep over them as we lie there planning our next approach or argument.

An old fable tells about two monks who wanted to cross a swiftly moving river. A woman came up and also wanted to cross, but was afraid. One of the monks put the woman on his shoulders, walked her across, and set her down to go her way. The younger monk said, "You broke your vows. We are not supposed to touch women." The older monk said, "I have already set her down. You are still carrying her."[87]

This is the way we are with resentments, worries, and things we can't change. How much of the stuff that is still affecting our emotions and thoughts is useless weight that we could have set down long ago. This seems to be especially true with families and friends falling out over a perceived or real hurt. Carrying this block of ice between us and another person is heavy and leaves us with feelings frozen in time. It blocks us from joy and growth.

Why not set it down and begin to see the beauty of living again?

Strangely Warmed

Most of us have grown up with a concept of heaven. When we speak of such a place we often look or point up. Even the Bible makes reference to a dove descending, and the heavens opening up. Astronauts say that when we are in space, there is no sense of up and down. Up and down is an experience of gravity or point of reference. It is the same even if you were able to go to the very center of earth. Where then, would down be? All of this challenges our traditional concept of reference to heaven.

The point of this rambling musing is to say many of us have developed a belief in an existence beyond where we are now, a realm for our souls after death. It is a "place" where spirits reside. Do we ponder this location and form for our departed loved ones because of our need to see them again?

---

87. Gerrold, "Zen."

Do their spirits actually exist in what we call eternity? I go with the majority and hope so.

More importantly, I like to believe that they are aware of us, and of what we experience and feel in our lives. I like to think anyone who has passed to this "place" has a heavenly pager that goes off when we think about them. At that moment, they feel our love. Even if we have questions or anger, they also know the love that lies under those feelings. When we think about them and make a connection of spirits, love flows back and forth.

I don't know. I was sitting on the porch in my nightly ritual of winding down before bed and this thought came to me. And as described by John Wesley, I felt "strangely warmed" by it. I do believe there are spirits watching over, under, and around us or we wouldn't survive some of the challenges we face in this journey.

Some might say this is simplistic. It gives me a sense of comfort. What about you?

Teachers and Educators

We often think of teachers as the ones who are in front of the classroom as we were getting our "larnin'". One definition of teacher is someone who gives lessons on a subject. I used to call this teaching style "dump truck teaching". They dump it out in lectures and notes on the board. Then they give a test so we can dump it back. Doesn't sound too exciting, does it? Don't label me as a cynic. I learned something from all my classroom experiences.

On the other hand, there are educators. They are defined as persons who teach, train, develop, inform, and coach. This last word, "coach" sets aside those who do more than just give out material. A coach gets involved with his or her students, and infuses excitement along with the desire to learn. We experience a dynamic presence, someone who truly loves what he/she is doing. We learn a lot from these vibrant transmitters of knowledge and experience.

I was blessed to reconnect with an educator I will never forget. I valued his love of education, and his passionate, dynamic style of teaching. He would float into the classroom, hop upon the desk, sit with his legs crossed Indian style, and begin to paint a picture of American History. Each day it was like going to the movies. We could see the scenes of the American

Revolution, forming and signing of the Constitution, the Civil War, tragedy and abuse of slavery, prohibition, etc.

I think his love of teaching, love for his students, and his general passion for life has kept him going. He was at our 50th high school reunion. You could feel the love and respect many of us shared for him as well as our general awe with the differences he made in our lives.

I hope each of you had the blessing of many such educators. Thank you, Mr. Doug Carico for making school and learning a joy for me!

Good Purpose

I was in a seminar years ago where the theme was "Speaking with Good Purpose." We hear anger, rage, negativity, prejudice, and complaining from all sides. A day doesn't go by before someone makes unhappy comments about someone or a situation. These aren't necessarily long discourses. Most are brief. However, the whole body experiences the effects of these darker thoughts and comments. Scientists say that every cell in our bodies has a connection with the brain. Therefore every cell can be affected by what goes on up top![88]

We would do well to cultivate not only speaking with good purpose, but also thinking and acting with good purpose. It is more work to create good habits than bad ones. I am not sure why. Maybe bad habits feed our egos. Therefore, when we focus on ourselves and what we want, we are naturally drawn to the quickest available source of satisfaction. Some call this "navel gazing."

Not only have I seen positive results for individuals who change their thinking, acting, and speaking to good purpose, but I also believe that the world can feel the impact, particularly if a lot of people are doing it.

When negativity arises within, we can use a process called "thought-stopping." Thought-stopping involves quickly stopping negative thoughts. Even though others can be annoyed or upset by it, we can physically yell out, "*stop*" if that's what it takes.

May your day and week be filled with the warm experiences of living with good purpose!

---

88. Lipton, "Food and Health."

Possibility

We have needs. These needs are programmed into our being. We have basic physiological needs such as food, water, sleep, etc. that are necessary to stay alive. Once these needs are met, we as creatures of the Ultimate Creator, have higher needs.

Most of us need to identify a purpose for being. Many are motivated when they are needed by others. Some of us contribute to society in other ways.

A lot of us dream of a major invention or event that would give us recognition. Some people accomplish such a dream, and it changes the way they live. If we compare ourselves to those with fame and celebrity who have made far-reaching contributions to the world, we may feel that we have nothing to offer. So we plod along feeling like a common person or nobody.

What we don't realize is that all of us contribute to life. We may not receive the Nobel Prize. However, our contributions are no less important or far-reaching. Most of us will never know the extent to which we affect the world. We may be a small pebble in the pond of life, but we can affect people we never meet in ways that change their world.

"Survival often depends on a specific focus, a relationship, a belief, or a hope balanced on the edge of possibility . . . ."[89] I am struck by the phrase, "the edge of possibility." Possibility is the candy store of life. The possibilities that make a difference in people's lives are limitless.

One man made a positive difference in the nursing home where he was a resident. He was still able to move around and speak to others. His spirit was positive. He loved to tell stories. He was filled with humor. The eyes of those who were distraught lit up by his presence and attention. It was such a simple thing in a small place on this planet, and yet powerful enough to make the difference in more than one person's day.

What are the possibilities that lie before you today?

Time

"We are all hostages of time. We each have the same number of minutes and hours to live within a day. . . ."[90]

---

89. Bailey, "Snail," 28.
90. Bailey, "Snail," 50.

Musings

I find it interesting that the same amount of time means different things to different people. Most of us have pursued a life that only seems to have value in the fast lane. If there are moments with no activity or we have to wait in line or in an office, we may fidget, drum our fingers, swing a leg or foot, shift from one side to the other, sigh often and loudly, roll our eyes, and flip through a magazine without really seeing anything. The next time you are in a situation with a group of people who have to wait, be an observer. Look at the kinetic energy pulsating around you. Hey, you may realize that you are part of this concert of broken chords!

In contrast to most of the population who are running on the treadmill of life, those who have been ill and confined to a bed seem to have an abundance of time. Time even seems to stand still.

I share this revealing quote from Elisabeth Tova Bailey, who was confined to a bed for a number of years with an illness that left her too weak to be able to lift herself up from the bed. She said about her visitors, "They would worry about wearing me out, but I could also see that I was a reminder of all they feared: chance, uncertainty, loss, and the sharp edge of mortality. Those of us with illnesses are the holders of the silent fears of those with good health."[91]

There are thoughts or lessons here. We all have the same amount of time in a day. Too little or too much time is all about attitude, not a measurement of the journey. Maybe our speed of living is driven by the fear of incapacitation or death. If so, we may be most aware of it in the presence of illness and dying.

If we can teach ourselves to be aware of our spirits or our attitudes, in any given moment the world will look different. We may also be able to minister to and love those who are ill with our total presence. Our chatter, fidgeting, and jerky movements bring no peace to someone needing to conserve energy, and they instill no peace in us.

May your fingers be steady, your leg and foot at rest, your butt still, your breathing even, your eyes focused, and your mind aware of who you are.

(And for more great lessons of life, read Elisabeth Tova Bailey's book, *The Sounds of a Wild Snail Eating*.)

---

91. Ibid., 251.

Waiting for the Worm

We live in techno society. I think it is important to look at the ways we are affected by that technology.

If we depend too much on technology, we can lose some of our creativity. We sit and are fed mindless but engaging entertainment. The brain is not involved other than being a dumping ground. We can often be compared to little birds sitting in the nest with our mouths open, waiting for techno mom to drop the worm down our throats. We stare at the television or other visual devices allowing the programmers to funnel whatever they choose into our brains. We often lose consciousness about what is happening to us, e.g., how the content may be subtly changing the way we think and act.

I have often wondered what would happen if some phenomenon, such as a huge sun spot, cancelled out all radio, television, and computer signals for a year. How would our lives change?

I suspect we would awaken our humanness with creative endeavors, healthy socialization, and learning to play again. We would become more aware. We would use things around us to invent and craft functional, aesthetic creations. We would be able to talk to people, look them in the eye, listen, and really hear them without the cell phone going off, and without being "zoned out" on an electronic screen.

In my youth, I spent a lot of time on projects with my father and grandfather. We didn't have any power tools. The garden was "tilled" by a mattock. We built most things with hammer, nails, and a hand saw. If we didn't have a tool for a specific task, we improvised. The camaraderie was priceless. I am suggesting that we remain in charge of ourselves rather than being controlled by our electronic devices. Remember the movie *Space Odyssey 2001* where "Hal" the computer took over the ship? Far-fetched? Maybe not.

Regaining creativity can improve both our mental health and our sense of self-worth. We are made in the image of the Creator which suggests that we too are creators. When I build a piece of furniture, capture a wonder of creation on film, or write about life, I experience a sense of satisfaction and well-being. It almost seems a contradiction that I use technology to get these thoughts to you! Yet, it is still about who is in control of your time.

Look at the delight and aliveness in children's eyes and bodies when they have drawn or made something with their hands. This is my picture of what it really means to be alive!

Musings

Potty Mouth

If I spoke "inappropriate" language growing up, I was said to have "potty mouth." Much to my dismay, "potty mouth" got washed with soap and it wasn't just a threat. It happened only once. To this day, I don't like the taste of soap!

Have we allowed some of what we read or watch as entertainment to reduce our moral grounding? Are we bored and allow what we might have called trash or tragedy at one point to become our entertainment? The more risqué the actions and language on television, books, movies, and conversation, the more audience attraction it seems to have. I admit to telling and enjoying off-color jokes. What I define as "off-color" often relates to the embarrassing foibles of human behavior. However, is there a difference between off-color and being vulgar? We all have to be careful not to be desensitized and conditioned by popular opinion that can lull us to go over the edge!

I am not advocating for any governing body to limit the freedom of speech. The censorship of material should be each individual's responsibility. Yet, it appears that what we call entertainment today could erode the moral fiber of society—or is that just something someone my age would say in any generation? I wonder what will be "exposed" five or ten years from now?

Even radio has become a medium to push the limits of FCC regulations. We have a label for those who do push those limits—they are called "shock jocks." What does that suggest to you? Is being shocked the stimulation we desire to battle our boredom? I don't think the creators of the Constitution took "freedom of speech" to mean saying anything you think.

My grandmother used to say, "Trash in, trash out." *Hmmm* . . . old-time wisdom makes a lot of sense.

Is the increase in violence across the world partly influenced by the trash talk and disrespect for others we see in our news and entertainment? A well-known carpenter said, "What goes into someone's mouth does not defile them, but what comes out of their mouth, that is what defiles them." (Matt 15:11)

I think the carpenter and my grandmother were wise people.

Badges of Life

I looked down at my hand the other day and noticed a dark spot. I became shockingly aware of an age spot. My initial response was, "Oh man, I am getting old and mottled like a piece of fruit that has set out too long!"

Then I thought, "Well, part of our goal is to make it to our senior years so why shouldn't there be signs of the aging process?" (Thank goodness I am not ready for Depends!) Why not look upon these spots as badges of experience, wisdom, and courage from living a full life. Maybe we can create a club, wear a sash, and call it "The Organization of Gray Aging Seniors," *o-gas*.

Aging gracefully reflects realization that you have given to the world and have contentment and joy in your contributions. I guess this is why I like films like *Star Wars*. Luke Skywalker had to earn his badges trusting his internal powers, living wisely, and going forth with courage. Another favorite series is *Indiana Jones*. Ah, the adventures and experience of living and surviving the challenges of life!

Each morning we awake to the possibility of an adventure. If we jump in with gusto, we will end up with the badges of distinction from those adventures—maybe even a few self-inflicted patches from hare-brained ideas!

Oh, I just found another one!

Wednesday Again

>Is it Wednesday again?
>I thought it was Thursday
>What happened to Friday, Saturday, Sunday, Monday, and Tuesday?

>I now know why the ole timers used to say, "Why I remember just yesterday!"
>Yesterday being years and years ago
>What happened to the real yesterday?
>And all those days in between

>I worked all those years trying to follow the urging of the sages
>"Be in the moment" they said
>Now I don't have to work so hard
>My brain does the work for me

Musings

I love to read books
After I have read the third one
I can't remember for the life of me what the first one was about
Well, I guess I don't have to spend money buying books
I will keep the three I have and go back to the first one and enjoy it again!

They took the keys to my car from me
Said it wasn't safe to drive anymore
It was an answer to my prayers
Now I have a full time chauffeur

I guess age has its advantages
It doesn't take much to make me happy
And when they accuse me of doing something
I don't have to worry about feeling guilty
Because I certainly don't remember doing it!

Today is Wednesday
I'll make it a good day,
For all I know tomorrow will be Wednesday again.

—Edward L. Boye, 2013

Look Before You Leap

Air Force One was flying across the country. There were six people aboard, the pilot, the President, the Vice President, the Secretary of State, an elderly priest, and a young man going to hike in the mountains. The plane developed engine trouble, and the pilot said, "We are going to have to parachute." To their dismay, they found only five parachutes. The pilot grabbed one and jumped saying, "I am not going down with this plane". The President said, "The country needs me," and jumped with a parachute. The Vice President said he needed to be there to back up the President and took another parachute. The Secretary of State picked up a parachute and jumped, saying "I am one of the smartest people in the cabinet and the country certainly needs me." This left the old priest, the young man and the last parachute. The old priest said, "Son, I've had a long and productive life. You take that last parachute and go." The young man said, "Don't worry, we can both survive. That smartest person in the country just grabbed my backpack!"

This story fits the old adage, "Look before you leap." We spend a lot of time passing around information that we don't take time to check out. We often say we are too busy to spend the time. As a result, we unintentionally perpetuate hearsay.

What sources do you trust for the truth? I saw two trusted fact-checking organizations print opposing opinions. We may be gullible and assume that whoever is sharing something has gotten it from a reliable source. Does this make us propagators of misinformation?

Sometimes we pass something on that we hope makes us look smart and knowledgeable, only to end up with egg on our faces when the truth is uncovered.

It's probably wise to check things out before we speak. When I taught Psychology, I encouraged my students to engage in "critical thinking" as they wrote their assignments, to make sure what they were saying was reliable. Hearsay can distort reality, ruin lives, and perpetuate ignorance.

"Know the truth, and the truth will set you free!" (John 8:32)

Treasures in Plain Sight

How many times have we missed an opportunity because we weren't paying attention—or held back because we weren't bold enough to act immediately? Not paying attention can cause us to lose treasure and opportunity. "Snooze and you lose," as they say.

Once there was a man who owned a farm and, because of economic difficulty, had to start selling things. Finally, all that was left was the farm itself, which eventually was sold. The front door of the farmhouse wouldn't stay open so the previous owner had placed a rock at the base of it. The new owner was sitting in a chair one day, and noticed sunlight coming through the center of the rock. The next day he took the unusual rock to a geologist to discover that it held one of the largest diamonds ever found. The former owner's solution to his economic problems was right in front of him.

Treasures are not just material objects. We fail to find the beauty in a moment or in a person because we are too wrapped up in something. It is as if our eyes are turned inward, seeing and worrying about all of the things reeling across our minds like a never-ending movie. We miss treasures in plain sight.

Musings

We often know that others aren't listening when we see the glazed-over look in their eyes. We experience it ourselves when we have driven ten miles and don't remember any of the drive. Or we wake up in a hospital bed and wonder how we got there!

Jesus said something about our hearts holding the true treasures of life. (Matt 6:19-20) I think we will be pleasantly surprised by listening to our hearts more often. Our hearts "see" what the eyes miss. It can be like the beauty of the sun shining through a diamond!

Best of Everything

I remember the first time I had the means to buy a new car. I didn't just go to the dealer's lot and pick from what he had. I pored over brochures with all the options and listed what I wanted. It was like I was designing my own personal vehicle. I sat with the dealer and he made out an order and sent it to the manufacturer. It took weeks for the car to arrive. When I drove it off the lot, I was "on top of the world". I wanted to show everyone. I washed and waxed it about once a week. All of this lasted about eight weeks. Then the car became just transportation, and I was off looking for the next "want."

I have been excited when planning trips to exotic places in the world. I have taken a lot of pictures. I enjoyed what I saw and experienced. But I came home and started planning the next trip. We had picture albums that collected dust. Why not get them down occasionally and relive the experience? Or convert them to a digital file and use them as a screen saver on our computer? But even now, we can get so caught up in answering email or searching the web that we don't even see them.

Some of this is programmed into us. We are gatherers, hunters, and creatures of migration by nature—a program that was there at one time for our survival. Some of us have not updated the program so it doesn't show the overabundance of things and experiences we have had. The old program has a bug in it now that confuses *need* and *want*. If we are hung up on always looking ahead to what we still want, there is no way to see, savor, and enjoy what we gained from our longings in the past.

Take a few moments each day to look around at what you have already gathered. Don't just look, but gaze at it, taking in its detail, remembering when you first got it, and why you longed for it at the time. Relive your journeys by looking at the pictures, and remembering why you captured that particular scene. It is especially fun to do this with the person or persons who were with you on the trip.

"Those who are happy don't have the best of everything; they just make the best of everything they have."[92]

Iron-Clad Contract

The plot in a lot of books and movies, especially drama, mysteries, and thrillers, is based on a good person or group going up against a villain. Often the villain tries to defeat the good side by enticing someone from the good side to be a spy. This person is lured by promises of power and money. They do the footwork for the mastermind, but in the end the villain "snuffs" them—that's gangster talk for eliminating them permanently! There is truly no honor, trust, or happy results among thieves. The "schnook" who thought he was really onto the "big one" is always shocked when he realizes that he is going to lose everything. We know one, by the name of Judas.

There is a good guy who promises better than riches, power, and fame. He promises eternal life. What more can we ask for? We have been looking for the fountain of youth for centuries, and it is right before us all the time. We just have to go through a process called life to get there. To receive this gift of eternal life, we don't have to do anything immoral, illegal, or destructive. There are no hidden motives. Our position is secure no matter what we have done. We aren't punished for failing. All we have to do to receive this free gift is to open our hearts. The one who offers this was also offered fame and fortune early in his journey by a villain. He chose to reject it.

I guess this promise of a free gift is a difficult thing for us to understand. We even have a saying, "There is no free lunch." We live in a world where there always seem to be strings attached to what people want from us. We discover, after the fact, the hidden costs. Sometimes we are baited to come into a store and walk out with something we didn't expect to buy. We learn that people aren't always honest. It is no wonder that we don't believe that we can "drink from a fountain" that promises eternal life.

Read the contract, if you are having difficulty accepting this deal of all deals. It is called the New Testament.

---

92. Author unknown

Musings

Overwhelmed!

A man was hired for a job. When he got to the job site, the boss gave him a spoon and told him to move a mountain of sand to the other side of the lot. The man said, "How in the world am I going to get all that sand from here to there with just a spoon?" The boss said, "One spoonful at a time."

Sometimes our lives feel that we only have a spoon to do all we think we have to do in a day. Some mornings we wake up with a sense of dread. We are already expending energy thinking about the day ahead. But that energy can be applied to its demands.

How can we get done all that we think we have to do? We can't. If we try, we will hurt ourselves, if not immediately, then in the long run.

Sometimes making a prioritized list helps put things in perspective, rather than letting the entire so-called "have tos" make us feel like our brains are heavy with grains of sand. I find great satisfaction in drawing a line through each task completed.

It is important to focus on the task at hand without thinking ahead to the next one. The tasks will get done faster and better when we take our time. Spilling the sand only means we have to stop and clean it up. If we were to become ill, injured or die, it wouldn't matter anyway.

I see this familiar statement from Jesus in a different light: "Truly I tell you, if you have faith as small as a mustard seed, you can say to this mountain, "Move from here to there," and it will move. Nothing will be impossible for you." (Matt 7:20). I don't think he meant that it would happen immediately. A mustard seed is like a grain of sand. With persistence and faith, what feels like the mountains of life can be moved, even with a spoon.

"Think not of the amount to be accomplished, the difficulties to be overcome, or the end to be attained, but set earnestly at the little task at your elbow, letting that be sufficient for the day."[93]

What is not completed today is always there tomorrow. And if there isn't a tomorrow, it won't matter anyway!

Our Best Teacher

It is amazing that we spend so much time chiding ourselves over the mistakes we have made in life. Growing up with a limited attention span and hyperactivity, I made my share of mistakes (and probably enough for

---

93. Osler, Canadian Physician, 1849 to 1919.

several others). I used to be embarrassed, shamed, and full of regret about those mistakes.

I was sharing with my brilliant wife about how amazed I am to be able to focus enough to create these musings. She said, "Who better than someone who lives with impulsivity and has made plenty of mistakes to offer the rest of us the wisdom learned from those mistakes?"

My perspective of those mistakes has changed from regret to revelation. Mistakes are an opportunity to learn better ways to think and act differently next time. They may be our best teacher.

If we could all look at them this way, we wouldn't spend so much time chastising ourselves. There are enough other people around who have a need to do that anyway. I have said for years, "There are no mistakes, only lessons." Saying it, though, isn't believing it. It takes some soul-searching and deep reflection not to be dragged down by something that doesn't turn out like you thought it would. We must turn around what most of the world sees as a negative to an opportunity of discovery. "Wow, what can I learn from this?"

May you realize that your mistakes are the road to wisdom both for you and any others who use the opportunity you've given them to learn.

Resentment

Carrying resentment toward another person about a negative experience from the past will affect your whole life. It can even affect your attitude and actions toward those who are a part of your life today, especially your loved ones. It can block understanding and compassion, cause physical illness, and make your outlook on life a dark and bitter one.

To hold resentment is to be controlled by it. We give it power to affect how we feel and act. Resentments are like old wounds that ache when we least expect it. Someone's comment, an attitude, or a look may remind us of the person who wounded us.

We may not even be aware that resentments developed in childhood can continue throughout our lives. Our negative attitudes may pop up when we least expect them, e.g. causing us to be short with someone, avoid being around them, or sabotaging a situation. We may be fearful of facing resentments toward our parents. We are told to honor our father and mother. We are also told to forgive, and forgiving is to let go. One of the most difficult things we have to do in life is to stop carrying around our hurts and bitterness toward others.

Some get a payoff by showing the scars for all to see. "Look at me. I have been a victim of someone who was supposed to love me." How grim is that outlook on life? Or we want to hurt them as badly as we hurt. Many times we cover up our resentments with things like addiction(s), weight gain, controlling others, playing the victim, and/or being greedy because we were cheated.

One can see a visible change in demeanor in the people who finally are able to forgive, to let go of hurt and bitterness toward someone, and to allow themselves to no longer be controlled by their wounds. They look lighter. There is a sparkle in their eyes. An aura of happiness surrounds them. Truly, a burden has been lifted.

How does one find the strength and determination to let go of that which is doing them, those around them, and the world no good?

Sometimes it takes working through those wounds with a professional. It may take being able to see good qualities as well as the resentments toward the person one resents. It often takes prayer and immersing one's self in positive thoughts and energy. Basically, it takes work! The encouraging news is that we are not alone in this endeavor. We are told there will be an "advocate" with us forever.

Silent Shame

He stood with the others
    Excited about the possibility of being a star
Two "captains" were chosen
    Two teams to make
He waited with visions
    Of Babe Ruth and Ted Williams
First Chuck was chosen
    Everyone wanted him, he was the best
Then Bret was next
    He was the fastest runner around
Each time he looked directly
    At the captains, in hope he'd be next
But the process went on until

>   He was standing alone
>   Someone said to the other side
>   With the last pick
>   "Ha you get *him*
>   You are sure to lose now!"
>   And suddenly he didn't want to
>   Be seen anymore.

—Edward L. Boye, 2000

Great Expectations

Expectations can lead to a lot of grief and disappointment. We *expect* someone to act or respond a certain way. We *expect* to get our fair share of whatever.

We put a lot of energy into expectations. Expectation can be egotistical and arrogant. It is like saying, "I am in charge and I expect you to . . . ." William Shakespeare probably says it best,

> "Oft expectation fails, and most oft there
> Where most it promises; and oft it hits
> Where hope is coldest; and despair most fits."[94]

In our society we often expect the best. Expectations are part of our definition of success. Maybe they are also why so many people feel defeated, stressed, and depressed. "It just didn't work out the way I expected it would."

Having goals and dreams gives us hope and takes away despair. But having expectations comes more from the self-serving ego than from the spirit of love and acceptance.

"Truly loving another means letting go of all expectations. It means full acceptance, even celebration of another's personhood."[95]

Having realistic goals and dreams motivates us and gives us hope. Goals and dreams leave room for accepting "what's so" when we arrive at the destination of our hope.

---

94. Shakespeare, "Ends Well," 145–147.
95. Casey, Author and Speaker.

Musings

To hope is to look forward to each day. Without hope, what is left? We just exist in a state of cynicism and despair.

To dream is like painting a beautiful picture. Dreaming gives color to life. All dreams don't have to be serious. Sometimes it is fun to dream what it would be like to fly like a bird, be a super hero, or walk on the moon. These are fantasy dreams of that little girl or boy who still resides within.

Goals and dreams (realistic and fantasy) fill us with the bright light of joy. Maybe we will feel like we are flying.

Can You Hear the Quiet?

Have we created a pace of life and busyness that keeps us from hearing the quiet? How can we hear quiet, you say? Quiet means there is no noise, no sound, right? Not necessarily. How would you know what the quiet sounds like if you don't take time or know how to listen?

When my wife and I first moved from our previous home to our home in the mountains on a lake, we were lying in bed before going to sleep and I said, "Do you hear that?" She said, "I don't hear anything." And I replied, "Precisely."

We are uncomfortable with silence. It means we aren't doing something, and we are told that not doing something is being lazy or unproductive. Taking time to find a place to sit or lie and be silent will probably feel like tearing our skin away from life's essential elements—the expectations, doingness, and material surroundings.

There are spaces between sounds. We can actually step outside sounds, even in a noisy city, by being present to ourselves. It is sort of like stepping out of our ears and observing what is going on, as weird as that sounds. We do it when we are preoccupied with internal thoughts in the midst of all that is going on around us. Yet, even these thoughts are also a form of noise. I call them "monkey mind".

To really listen to the spaces between the sounds, we have to stop and observe. We have to be totally aware of the moment. To hear the in-between, we have to separate ourselves from the physical, and let the soul listen.

It is almost impossible to go into anyone's house and not hear ambient sounds from all the electronics. As I sit here typing, I hear the timer for the lamp ticking away, the dryer whirring, the keyboard clicking, and some other distant hum.

We are sometimes struck by the sudden quiet when our electrical power goes out. People can hear each other at a deeper level during these times. We may even see things that we had not noticed because the noise distracted us.

We must intentionally make time to hear the quiet between the sounds. Who knows, maybe you will hear the whisper of angels' wings.

Little Teacher, Big Lessons

Every morning after I have written a musing, I have my breakfast and feed my four footed, ten pound ball of fur, who then goes to the door, sits and looks at me with an expression of, "Well?" So we put on her harness and out the door we go. I, with my long legs, take about five steps and am brought up short. "Little Teacher," better known as Abbie, has stopped in the middle of the driveway to stretch, breathe in the scents, and look around. I am "chomping at the bit" to head up the steep driveway. Finally, she decides it is time to move on. We reach the top of the hill after several more stops.

I view the morning trips as exercise. Abbie looks at them as immersing herself in her surroundings. She stops frequently, checking out each bug and leaf, listening, observing and smelling. Only then she looks up at me and says, "Ok, you can move now."

We walk pretty much the same route every day. It is only about a mile round trip, same houses, same trees, same weeds, and same road. And yet they are not the same. She has taught me this by being excited about making our "new" journey each day. If something is there that hasn't been there before, she points it out. When she hears a vehicle coming our way, she sits in the road to see who it is, as if every person in the vehicle is important. I have forgotten that, actually, they are. She is determined to teach me to look at what seems to be a familiar scene, to find how it changes day to day. New weeds seem to grow overnight. Leaves change shape. There are marks and places in the road that weren't there yesterday. She stops in front of a cabin that has a car in the driveway that wasn't there yesterday. She looks at me as if saying, "Let's wait awhile. Maybe they will come out and play."

"The whole earth is filled with awe at your wonders; where morning dawns, where evening fades, you call forth songs of joy." (Psalm 65:8)

Big lessons about small things from a small teacher.

The Wounded Caretaker

Guilt and anger are common feelings when someone suddenly becomes a caretaker. The person receiving care is also likely to have anger. Their feelings of anger may revolve around the indignities of needing help with personal functions, not being independent, having their privacy invaded, etc.

When life calls us to care for aging parents, we may have to make difficult decisions, e.g., taking their car keys away, taking over managing their finances, setting limitations, etc. Probably the most difficult is making the decision to put them in a personal care home.

Such obligations and decisions cause a tremendous strain. In most cases, the people we undertake to care for are our parents. They have been the pillars of our life or, in early life at least, the ones we depended on to survive. Having to become the "parent" of our parents can be difficult and painful.

We may be called to care for our spouses, which can include feelings of loss for aspects of the relationship that are no longer possible. Or we may be called to undertake the care of our adult or disabled children. We grieve over the loss of all that they are missing in life.

Often we feel guilt over making the necessary decisions for the wellbeing of the person we are caring for. Over time, the stress of making those decisions and the strain of giving daily care can lead to a buildup of anger. We may have to give up some of the routines and freedom in our own lives to be caretakers.

When we see others suffering, we are most compassionate and effective if we can identify our own wounds and suffering, and find ways to take care of ourselves. Acknowledgment of any guilt and anger can help us to a place of acceptance. Seek support from others so that you can have breaks without feeling guilty. Everyone under pressure needs periods of time out to at least "catch their breath". Talking with someone about the feelings and hurts that keep coming up can help. A good listener is essential.

May you be blessed with strength to love yourself and to continue to find love for those who must adjust to a more interdependent lifestyle.

Help in Time of Need

We are beings of energy. EEGs and EKGs measure the electrical energy of our brains and our hearts. We talk about burning calories and about building up lactic acid. All of these refer to burning energy.

Some people can see auras. An aura is a "field of subtle, luminous radiation surrounding a person or object."[96] We radiate energy. When someone walks into a room, we can often *feel* the energy emanating from them. This is especially true with children. Have you ever wished we could bottle that energy?

I believe in a balance between rest and action, and yet there are times when we believe we must keep on going. You know the kind of day—it's difficult to put one foot in front of the other. So, where do we get the energy to do it?

How can we get an "extra burst" of energy? When the need arises, the body can generate adrenalin, giving us more endurance. Stress generates both chemical and neurological signals to allow us to "fight or flight" situations that offer a threat to our well-being.

We also draw energy from others, nature, and our surroundings. Energy comes from feeling needed and being loved. Air, trees, plants, and water also produce energy that can affect us in positive ways. The experience of stepping outside a building, taking fresh air into our lungs, and feeling nature can be invigorating. Listening to music that brings *nature* inside can be helpful.

Finally, knowing we are being supported spiritually can be a comfort. Even if we aren't aware of it, spirit guides may be helping us endure a difficult situation. Perhaps we feel an inward knowing and motivation in our heart that helps us. Examples might include a couple who gets up at all hours of the night with a newborn or a caregiver who dispenses medicine every two hours to someone with an illness. Sleep is interrupted. These daily routines can be a huge energy drain, and yet, these people find the energy to keep doing what is needed.

"In the same way, the Spirit helps us in our weakness. We do not know what we ought to pray for, but the Spirit himself intercedes for us through wordless groans." (Rom 8:26)

---

96. Wikipedia, "aura."

Maybe the "groans" emanating from us during these times of dwindling energy are coming from the Spirit! However, we must be careful not to blame the Spirit for all our groaning.

Peace and Quiet: Part I

When we asked my dad what he wanted for his birthday or Christmas, he always had the same answer, "peace and quiet." Looking back, I can understand why. For one, he had three children three years apart in age. We contributed to the chaos, surrounding him with our hyperactivity and not focusing enough energy on making contributions to the family's survival.

He served churches as a United Methodist minister. Being a pastor is probably one of the most challenging and difficult jobs around.

What is peace? Do we want peace permanently? Is it possible to live in today's world from a place of peacefulness?

Often we associate peace with cessation of war between countries. Could we call this an external peace? We are somewhat removed from it, sitting in our comfortable chairs watching the news of war on television or reading about it in the newspaper. The extent of our involvement may be in sending cards and care packages to soldiers, praising them when we see them. Yet, we are removed from the chaos of war.

Another type of peace is "peace of mind." We seek internal peace to soothe pain, struggle, or feelings of frustration. We want to feel no pressure or turmoil, just like my dad was seeking when he wanted "peace and quiet."

We may not be able to go to Afghanistan, Iran, or North Korea, or directly influence the powers that be toward external peace. When we are at peace with ourselves, we are able to be more open and accept where others are in their journey. Our own commitment to having peaceful and respectful relations with others is a pebble in the pond that can lead to a ripple effect around the world.

It is obvious as we look at the news about our own country that we feel tension and see turmoil. If we focus on creating peace in our personal relationships at home, at work, and with our neighbors, we are setting up positive energy to touch the lives of others, who touch the lives of others, who touch the lives of others, etc.

The song, "Let There Be Peace On Earth . . . and let it begin with me," says it all.

"We can never obtain peace in the outer world until we make peace with ourselves."[97]

Peace and Quiet: Part II

Do we want peace all the time? Being calm and blissful all the time may not be possible for most of us in traditional lifestyles. I traveled around the country making speeches and leading workshops for large audiences. Right before I had to face the crowd, I would have sweaty palms and anxiety I could feel from my toes to my finger tips. It wasn't crippling, but it was noticeable and perhaps necessary—I was exposed and vulnerable in the middle of that stage. What I call "creative tension" is natural for me when I want to do my best. It is the desire to give the group the best information and experience that I can so they can make a difference in the quality of their life.

A certain amount of tension can motivate us. Challenges help us grow in experience and wisdom. When we make amends to someone we have wronged, we often feel internal unrest which drives us to restore peace between us.

If it's not likely most of us can sustain strong peaceful feelings all the time, what should we aim for? I try to balance periods of peace with my times of creative tension. It often includes spiritual growing pains.

Feeling internal turmoil about something in our lives may be a sign that we need to restore a higher level of peace, whether the turmoil is due to something we've done or actions of others. Some endure anxiety about a situation as if they're carrying around a cactus with bare hands. It is a constant painful burden. Feeling peaceful again is to realize and let go of the pain the situation is causing. We must also clean up the wounds.

"Some tension is necessary for the soul to grow; we can put that tension to good use. We can look for every opportunity to give and receive love, to appreciate nature, to heal our wounds and the wounds of others, to forgive, and to serve."[98]

---

97. Dalai Lama, Tibetan Buddhist, 1935 to present.
98. Martin, "Life's Door," 304.

Musings

The Wizard of Widgets

I was in a theater the other evening for a concert with a symphony orchestra and a popular singing duo. There were around 1000 seats in the theater. We were sitting in the Loge, the forward balcony. I bent over the rail, and I was astonished by a surreal scene: nearly every third person had their head down looking at little blue light rectangles. They seemed oblivious to being at an event that was beautiful, spiritual, and wonderful.

If you allow your soul to savor the moment and contemplate the intimate connection between two different genres of music, you will be yourself transported to an enchanting place outside ordinary everyday life.

Yet, there were these "human doings" staring at small backlit LED screens as if they were slaves to an unseen wizard. It reminded me of the wizard's final discovery in the movie *Wizard of Oz*. He wasn't what he projected to be. Could we be captivated by technology that we will find out isn't as grand as we at first thought—one so captivating that we miss the beauty of life around us?

I have no objection to cell phones. I have one of the latest models myself. However, when mine becomes like a third arm, I'm sure I'm missing some of the beauty of living. I have seen people allowing them to interfere with intimate conversations, significant meetings, and the enjoyment of eating. Do they also distract others from the spirit of the moment when they insistently announce that you are being summoned?

Are we fearful to miss some bit of information? Are we desperate for connection with others, albeit at a safe distance? Cell phones are a tool of the so-called "social network." Is it possible to connect with someone and at the same time isolate others standing right in front of you?

Stop and listen to the music. It is a magic carpet ride to an enchanted place.

Thorns and Clay

Life brings us good days and bad days. The average person encounters most days as ordinary and typical. Then there are others who have to face battles every day because of a mental or physical challenge. Paul must have had such a challenge, as he called it "a thorn in my flesh." We can only speculate what the thorn was but apparently it was with him constantly. He even prayed for God to remove it. Yet, he continued to make a difference.

Others who have to live with such physical or mental limitations have also prayed to get better, to have their thorns removed, and yet they are still there. Why do thorns continue to plague us when we could offer so much more to life without them? We may never know. That's just the way it is.

So if a thorn doesn't go away, what do we do? We can accept the challenge to learn how to contribute to life in spite of our limitations. We can learn to maintain a pattern of life that doesn't worsen the situation. We can do our best to relieve the pain, stress, anxiety, and depression. When a National League baseball manager was asked what he was going to do when his team was having a bad season, he said, "I'll manage!" So, mostly, we manage. Managing is looking for ways to improve life, finding ways to avoid what makes it more difficult, and continuing to maintain strength, hope, and faith. We get up and face another day aware of the constant "thorn in our side." We may have doubts, which isn't always a bad thing. There was the man with the epileptic son who asked Jesus to heal his son. Jesus said, "Everything is possible for one who believes." (Mark 9:15) The man responded, "I do believe, help me overcome unbelief." (Mark 9:24) We need help with our unbelief in the moments of our "dark night of the soul".

I wonder what I can learn about this day. Will I let my limitations defeat me or will I let them teach me?

We are all "jars of clay." We can be fractured, chips can be knocked out of us, and we can be scraped, marked, and etched. The strength of the jar depends on the potter. If we believe we have been created by the hands of a master potter, then our jars of clay are more malleable. We can smooth over the thorns or learn to incorporate them into our lives.

What holds our lives together when so much is thrown at us? We all need a Paul who is where we are or has been where we have been. It is very comforting to have someone who knows what we are going through to share our stories, to listen with compassion, or just to hold our hand.

Know that your thorns may be limiting. Yet, know that you can still make a difference in life, however small the differences may seem.

Oh, the Innocence of Childhood

After a hard rainstorm filled all the potholes in the streets and alleys, a young mother watched her two little boys playing in the puddles through her kitchen window. The older of the two, a five-year-old lad, grabbed his sibling by the back of his head, and shoved his face into one of the water holes. As the boy recovered and stood laughing and dripping, the mother ran towards them in a panic.

"Why on earth did you do that to your little brother?" she said as she shook the older boy's shoulders in anger combined with relief. "We were just playing *church*, Mommy," he said. "And I was just baptizing him, in the name of the Father, the Son and in the Hole-he-goes."

Watch out for children playing church!

May your day be seen through the eyes of a child.

I Wish

We are a country of dreamers. We spend a lot of time wishing for dreams to come true. Wishing rituals are a part of our lives. We toss coins into a fountain and squeeze our eyes shut, intensely focusing on an image hoped for. We fill our lungs to capacity, close our eyes, and attempt to blow out all the candles on a cake while making a wish. (This particular ritual isn't really fair for those of us with some years behind us. The candles increase and the lung capacity decreases!) The breast of a chicken bone is held tightly between two dreamers, each hoping for the larger piece of broken bone so their wishes will come true.

There are more unfilled wishes floating around than there are realizations of what we wish for. Maybe your wish is to travel to Italy, Ireland, or Paris. Not being able to fulfill those wishes the way we envision doesn't mean that we can't experience them in creative ways. We are smart and resourceful enough to find ways to move them from images in our brains to experiences.

Some pasta, a bottle of wine, a movie, and/or music, can transport us to Tuscany. Some soda bread, lamb stew, and a pint of Guinness with an Irish jig playing in the background, and we find ourselves in an Irish pub. Candlelight, violins, and slow dancing in the living room, with visions of the Champs-Elysees, and we are in Paris.

If you can actually take trips to great destinations, that is grand. Even planning and daydreaming of such experiences can be fun. However, if you can't go to these places, immersing yourself in a creation of your own can bring joy in the moment. It takes stepping out of the box. Your mind is going to tell you this is silly. Throw this limiting thinking to the wind and celebrate life.

Wow! What marvelous creatures we are! What gifts the First Creator has bestowed upon us!

Pack your bags of stodginess, put them in a closet, and travel light!

Bon Voyage

Whitewashing Fences

Sometimes we seem to get into a rut. We go through the same mundane routines day in and day out, like programmed robots. We get stuck in single-mindedness. Bored to tears, some of us find ways to numb our senses as we plod along. Unfortunately, those numbing resources—often alcohol, pills, or even anger—rob us of the opportunities for joy-filled living.

My father was a master at turning a dull job into an adventure. One time after applying wax to a floor, he let us sit on an old quilt while he pulled and swung us around the hardwood floor to polish it. Sometimes it takes ingenuity to make mundane tasks fun.

If you read Tom Sawyer as a child, you will remember Tom's cunning in getting the fence whitewashed. He created an adventure for the other boys, and then thoroughly enjoyed watching it play out. He had made painting the fence sound so enticing that he was able to trade turns painting for the other boys' prized possessions. Even those bits of broken glass, a dog collar, a one-eyed cat, marbles, and other objects of interest for boys that age, were filled with possibilities.

Stepping back from our mundane activities and looking at them from different perspectives allow us to come up with creative and enjoyable ways of getting the task done. I suppose God had a blast creating the earth. And I am sure God is still amused at how we go about our lives. I see God is sitting on a barrel watching us "whitewash fences," some having fun while others are dulled by forgetting that we have been given the gift of creating new perspectives.

Life demands much of us, and those demands can be lessons and exciting adventures with a little forethought.

"Creativity is piercing the mundane to find the marvelous."[99]

---

99. Moyers, American Journalist, 1934 to present.

Musings

The Drive to Control

We feel a need to control people when we are fearful and insecure. We want them to agree with us, understand why we feel the way we do, and change to our way of thinking.

The acronym *"jaded"* describes some of the elements of our attempts to control someone:

- We work hard *justifying* our position. "It makes sense. Can't you see that?"
- We will *argue*, which drowns out the views of others.
- We are *defensive*, which puts a wall between ourselves and others.
- We have to *explain* our position to get the other person to "see reason."
- We are *determined* to win.

We can become jaded by verbal repetition, cynicism, callousness, and insensitivity. We attempt to wear others down in order to control them.

We feel if others accept us, adopt our way of thinking, and concede we are right, we will feel secure. This is a grand illusion. It is a bottomless pit. If we are not satisfied with ourselves, no amount of agreement is going to satisfy our insecurity.

There is a term in psychology called "bracketing." It means that we are willing to set aside our thoughts, responses, and opinions, and listen to another person with focus and an open attitude. To be willing to "bracket" and be open to differing opinions, we must feel good about ourselves and secure in our being. And sometimes the differing opinions we receive can give us new insight into life and can make our view of life and living richer.

We have been told that we are parts of a whole, with each part [person] as valuable as the next. Each part may be different, with different purposes in life and different views, but no one is more important than the other. (1 Cor 12:12–31) This sense of community and cooperation among many produces a "well oiled machine" that makes the journey a better one.

Know that you are okay just the way you are. The only way out of the fear that insecurity brings is to risk being open to the thoughts and views of others. There are gifts there, waiting to be received by an open mind once we let go of trying to control others.

The Charmed Ones

We often believe that there are people around us who lead charmed lives. We may look at someone and think that they flow through life with very few problems. They look like they are at peace and never seem to struggle. We are often more aware of them when we are having a difficult time.

I attended a meeting the other day where we shared some personal writings. I heard at least two persons share part of their journey of pain. I hurt for them and for me. When they read what they had written, it felt like something I had experienced and written about in my own diary.

In my counseling practice, I would often see a new client walk through the door looking like they were in complete control. But then I would hear about their fears and anxiety. I used to think physicians were people who were very sure of themselves and the work they were doing. One of my clients was a young physician who became anxious when he had to see clients over a period of time. He was so compassionate that he couldn't be objective. He carried their stress with him. Through therapy he discovered that he could still practice and avoid this cycle. He became an excellent emergency room physician where the contacts were brief. He was still compassionate, but able to let each case go as he went to attend to the next.

We are not alone on this journey that at times brings us confusion, frustration, and pain. When we read the Bible or any book that reveals someone's walk "through the valley," we find the struggles of their journey. However, reading about them seems far removed from where we sit. When we are in an intimate setting with another human being who is sharing from the heart, the reality of our communion with each other awakens us from our illusions. It doesn't help me understand pain and suffering any better, but it does make me realize that likely most of us experience the same struggles.

"Do not believe that the one who seeks to comfort you lives without difficulty the simple and humble words that sometimes help you. His life contains much grief and sadness and he remains far behind you. Were it not so, he would not have found those words." [100]

---

100. Rilke, *Letters*, 83.

Open Mouth . . .

Sometimes our mouths speak before our brains think. Why is that? Our mouths can't operate unless the brain sends the message. I have a friend who once said, "Light travels faster than sound. This is why some people appear bright until you hear them speak." We are in such a hurry to get our thoughts and opinions out that we speak before we have time to think about what we are about to say. This, unfortunately, is a common practice.

Most words that we speak aren't important anyway. They seem to be a form of filibuster to keep others from jumping in before we can illuminate them with our "brightness." "A man [or woman] of knowledge uses words with restraint, and a man [or woman] of understanding is even-tempered." (Proverbs 17:27)

Have you ever been in a group where one person is quiet? That person is just listening. In a pause in the chatter, the person speaks, and the whole group is astounded by the wisdom in a few simple words. He [or she] is a man [or woman] of few words, but when they speak, they make sense.

When writing we must go back and reread, make corrections, move phrases and sentences around, and correct our spelling to make it easier for others to understand our message. This is called editing. Unfortunately, we may not edit ourselves as we speak our thoughts and beliefs. At times we come across sounding foolish.

Patience to process our words before we share them takes practice and a sense of confidence that we will have our time to be heard. Since we are so conditioned to keep the words rolling, we need help to change this habit. The words that come to mind as I write are: "Let the words of my mouth, and the meditation of my heart, be acceptable in thy sight, O Lord, my strength and redeemer." (Psalm 19:14)

Oh, if we could only grab some of our words and stuff them back in our mouths.

Speak with good purpose.

Not What It Seems

Some years ago, I attended a men's workshop. One of the participants had a big belt with spikes on it; he had tattoos up both arms and probably elsewhere, a shaved head, and arms that looked like they could rip the door off a car. He was downright scary-looking. I thought, this guy is probably a Hell's Angel. What is he doing in a self-improvement workshop? Later, as I talked to one of the other attendees, the subject of the tattooed guy came up. You will be surprised what he did for living? He worked in a day care center! One of the guys who knew him said, "Yeah, the kids just love him. They crawl all over him as he sits in the floor playing with them."

What I was doing was prejudging him. I was prejudiced. And I thought I was a pretty open and accepting person. But I had categorized him in my mind before I knew him personally. How often do we do we see someone and immediately put the person in a box, wrap it up, and put a label on it? We are told when we are growing up, "Don't judge a book by its cover." We are also familiar with Jesus' admonition not to judge others.

But often we are too quick to count certain people as not good enough to be one of us "decent" human beings. Sounds pretty harsh when put that way, doesn't it? We may be missing opportunities to meet some solid, down-to-earth folks, persons who carry decency in a "strange wrapper."

Take time to look into someone's soul. You may be pleasantly surprised at what you see.

Living with the Enemy

I am working at eliminating the concept and word "enemy" from my life. Of course, there are people I am not fond of. They include people I don't want to be around, people who have acted hatefully toward me, and people who have taken advantage of me in my journey. My immediate reaction to them includes labeling them as a hated enemy, wishing them ill will, and considering revenge for their behavior.

What good does this do? Most of the time, we keep those feelings to ourselves. So who does it damage the most? We are putting out negative energy that only creates more negative energy, and this affects everyone. For those who can remember Al Capp's comic strip Li'l Abner, we are sort of like the character Joe Btfsplk who always had a dark rain cloud over his head. Instantaneous bad luck befell anyone unfortunate enough to be in his vicinity. Joe was a very lonely little man.

Fredrick Buechner, the American writer and theologian says, "For instance, if we're not ready yet to change passionate hate for somebody into passionate love, we can start by wishing people well whom we don't much

Musings

like, and it's hard to do that for long without developing a kind of grudging affection for them along the way. It's not much, but it's at least a start."[101]

Changing the way we think changes the world around us. Thoughts and words have a strong influence on whether we are sending out positive energy or contributing to the already over-abundance of negativity in the world.

So I want to say with the greatest sincerity and passion, "I do not have any enemies, just persons who desperately need my attempts at understanding, patience, and prayers, or to whom I at least wish good things."

If we would all adopt this mantra, do you think we would see a difference in our world? I've had numerous experiences seeing someone's spirit bring about attraction or repulsion. If some of us can avoid labeling certain people as enemies, and can see them as folks who hurt so badly that they have hate-filled lives, it might just be contagious. They need our prayers.

Simple Love

> As I sit in the Creator's cathedral
> I suddenly become aware of being loved
> The trees stand as majestic guardians
> bending in compassionate attention
> They offer their deep green foliage
> as if bringing gifts to a king
> The rich earth cradles my presence
> offering the security that its firmness brings
> Upon the wind's gift of scents
> I am carried back to former times
> Those same gossamer breezes caress my soul
> acknowledging the deep love that is always present
> I am sung a beautiful aria by a feathered spirit
> that feels like a tonic to a battered soul.
> Love is present in this cathedral
> and always has been
> We must take time to enter its enchanted space
> and then we experience truly unconditional love.

—Edward L. Boye, 2011

101. Buechner, *Whistling*, 72.

Our Unwieldy Body

Being a teenager is difficult. A lot of changes occur in their bodies, creating awkward and embarrassing moments. Some body parts grow faster than others. Arms suddenly shoot out and hang to the knees like a Neanderthal's. Feet are so big they can't be picked up without falling over them. Pimples are all over the place, like the plague of boils. Then there is the one-track mind looking forward to sex.

Being a "grey-ager" is fraught with similar issues of awkwardness. Some body parts slow down sooner than others. Your brain says, "Run," and your body says, "Yeah, right!"

Our bodies actually start shrinking. I was once six feet two inches tall. I am now six feet. Our bodies may shrink, but our feet seem to stay the same and look like those of the mythical forest creature, Sasquatch! Our arms begin to inch down toward our knees again. Age spots must be scar tissue equivalent to the plague of boils during teen years. Then there is the one track mind trying to remember sex.

Ah, isn't life a wonder!

Labor Day

I enjoy oxymorons, "jumbo shrimp," "bittersweet" or "silent scream." Our attempt to describe life is often "explicitly ambiguous." We attempt to express our wit with "morbid humor", and then we think we are "seriously funny." Sometimes our explanations to others create "harmonious discord." We go to the polls to vote for an "honest politician" who tells us that under their leadership things will be "tax free." If we believe that, we have achieved a state of being called "astutely gullible."

So while we are "here and there," enjoying this "working holiday," maybe we will achieve some "initial results." We may even have some "uninvited guests." We can greet them with "lukewarm enthusiasm," although we are probably being a "little deceptive."

I guess we will be "wise fools" to the "living end"!

The Whole Picture

The other day I was driving down the road, and a guy came around me and cut back into the lane just under my bumper. My immediate thought was to hit the horn for a long blast. I was filled with thoughts like, "Who does he think he is, endangering my life like that?" "Does he think he owns the road?" And I have other thoughts not fit for print. I had to tell myself, "It wasn't personal. He doesn't even know me."

It is too easy to criticize others when we don't see the whole picture. Everyone has a way of manifesting themselves in life based on their experiences—some not so healthy and others, potentially dangerous. If we could see through their eyes, we might not be so critical. Each person is where they are based on their experience, what they have been conditioned to believe, how they were treated in childhood, their self-perception, and even what state of mind they are in at the moment. Maybe they just fought with their partner, got fired from a job, or are just full of rage, and taking it out on anything that gets in their way.

Rather than increasing their destructive feelings, we have an opportunity to affect their lives in a positive way by having compassion toward them. To react or criticize will only add to the negative energy that keeps them from moving in a more positive direction. The love of acceptance we offer can plant the seeds for love and community.

Putting out positive energy toward that person, praying for them, and wishing them well may help them find some peace. It will make a difference in them, whether they are aware of what we are doing or not. We radiate energy, be it positive or negative that affects everything around us.

Remember the poem by Edwin Markham, "He drew a circle that shut me out, Heretic, rebel, a thing to flout. But love and I had the wit to win; we drew a circle that took him in."[102]

Smiles

A smile is an expression that is common to every culture. In most cases it is a sign of happiness, contentment, pleasure, joy, and amusement. There are many health benefits from smiling. It changes your mood. When you are feeling down, try smiling, and see if it doesn't lighten your mood. Smiling lowers blood pressure, boosts your immune system, and lifts the mood of those around you.

Smiling is often one of our early expressions. Some babies begin smiling from birth and others begin in the first few weeks, usually in their sleep.

---

102. Markham, "Hoe," American Poet, 1852 to 1940.

We think of babies crying immediately upon being born. Often this reaction helps them to begin breathing on their own.

So if this is an early expression for us, why don't we do more of it? It seems to be to be a great defense against the harshness of life. "A smile is a powerful weapon; you can even break ice with it."[103]

The reason for this "science lesson" is to remember that "You will never see a smiling face that is not beautiful!"[104] "Always remember to be happy because you never know who's falling in love with your smile."[105]

Grandchildren can do that for you!

I Can't Wait!

How often have we heard the words, "I can't wait!" Guess what? You are going to have to! Look at what St. James says, "Why, you do not even know what will happen tomorrow. What is your life? You are a mist that appears for a little while and then vanishes." (James 4:14)

The "I can't wait" state of mind focuses on the anticipated experience, making us miss every experience in between. Each day and each moment bring us something new. Each of these moments is truly a gift. Anticipation of a desired event or experience can give us moments of joy.

I was driving one day focusing on the next stop of many I had to make. Out the corner of my eye I saw three young deer in a kudzu patch just standing watching the road. As I flew by, I thought that would make a great picture. Photography is one of my hobbies. I continued to fly on by, giving up an opportunity for a "Kodak moment" and a chance to savor an experience of peace and beauty.

Be aware that life is like a mist that appears and then disappears. Let this motivate you to make each moment a chance to be filled with the gifts before us. It can give us a more peaceful countenance. If we learn this, we have obtained a bit more wisdom.

Each moment has something to offer our souls, no matter how common or mundane. There are so many ways to take time to look at the persons we love and the friends we have, to envelop them with all of our senses and spirit.

---

103. *Quote Garden,* Author unknown.
104. Ibid.
105. Ibid.

Musings

I have written about this theme a number of times. Maybe I need to remind myself to enjoy the gift of life with all its varied experiences, and to enjoy the people I tend to take for granted as I rush on by.

Health through Movement

Unfortunately, we are largely a sedentary country. We think exercise is pushing the buttons on the TV remote! I guess there are a lot of strong thumbs out there. This is especially true for the older generation. We often get more sedate as we age. We convince ourselves that we are too old to exercise or dance.

Focused breathing, dance, being aware of how your body feels in walking and even sitting is crucial for optimum health and longevity. This may sound contradictory, but lying down and feeling the earth under your body allows us to be aware of being grounded. Even the Bible alludes to the value of finding peace and comfort by being connected to the earth, "He makes me lie down in green pastures, He leads me beside still waters. (Ps 23:2)" Connecting to the earth before exercise is essential if we are to be reasonable about our limits or you will be lying down on a green carpet (or in my case, a red one) on a heating pad!

Science is confirming how valuable exercise is to our health. Many clinics and gyms offer the "Silver Sneakers" program, one many insurance companies support to encourage seniors to build strength, keep tendons flexible, and boost the immune system. We must overcome the mental chatter that causes us to make excuses instead of exercising. I recently saw a video about a ninety-four year-old woman ballroom dancing. Go to YouTube.com and type in Mathilda's Solo. It will amaze and inspire you.

Exercise not only opens your body and increases flexibility, but it can help us release unwanted emotions. We keep a lot of emotional pain in our bodies. Movement helps bring it to the surface so we can deal with it rather than carrying it around and turning it into physical pain.

The Orientals have known the benefits of exercise for centuries. In China and Japan you will see individuals and groups in parks practicing Tai Chi. This form of soft martial arts helps direct our flow of energy and focuses on slow and smooth body movements to increase our strength and relaxation.

May you lie down in green pastures and walk beside still waters with new vigor and a sense of peace. But first, you must get off the couch.

Living with Grace

What does it mean to live life with grace? When grace is mentioned, my first thoughts are of the prayers we offer over food or an elegance of movement, as in dance. To live each day with grace is a challenging endeavor—one that helps make sense of this journey we are on. Words often used to describe grace include elegance, beauty, politeness, and a spirit of generosity.

Each day is a fresh opportunity to fill oneself with a sense of grace. We can live each moment with these qualities in mind until they become a part of who we are. I believe we will want less, be less frustrated, and experience the fullness of life we all desire by becoming grace-filled.

I have been blessed to meet and know people who are filled with this elegance and generosity of spirit. They seem to glow with a warmth and acceptance that light up the room or the space they are in. Their actions and presence cause you to stop and know something is different and good.

Years ago, my father-in-law was dying with cancer and we were at his home. He spent most of the time in the bed too weak to move about. I was sitting at the dining room table, and saw him come from the back of the house in his robe and sit in his recliner in the next room with his back to us. In a few minutes he got up and came to the table with great effort to hand me an envelope. I opened it up to a birthday card and beautiful note from him. In the midst of his dying, he remembered that it was my birthday. I was speechless. Here is a person in great pain and weakness who takes time to find a card and give it to me! He died a week later. He was this person I am trying to describe, one who lived life with grace. (Another testament to that grace was the line of people from the funeral home out into the parking lot.)

This is who I want to be! Join me, and we can work on it together.

Thieves of Opportunity

Most of us try to make everyone happy. We don't like confrontation. We especially don't like to see people fight or be in conflict with each other. So we set ourselves up for trouble by trying to referee. Have you noticed that being a bridge often means you will be walked on from both sides? We have a difficult time allowing people to work out their differences. Getting between them can be like standing between the Hatfields and McCoys with their guns pointed at each other.

It is difficult to allow persons to grow by learning lessons from their own choosing. However, in most situations trying to rescue them is robbing them of the learning experience. How can they grow if they don't have experience? Making mistakes can be our greatest teacher.

This is an opportunity for them to learn to listen, to try seeing from the other person's perspective, and to learn negotiating skills. Sometimes, they don't succeed. They walk away carrying negative feelings, which is like living with a festering wound.

A sign of great love is being able to trust that everyone has the ability to take care of themselves. Besides don't we have enough of a challenge keeping ourselves out of trouble?

With time, thought, and experience, many take the opportunity to go back and clean up the bad feelings. The eighth step in twelve-step programs aiming toward a healthier and positive life says, "Made a list of all persons we had harmed and became willing to make amends to them all."[106]

When we allow others the opportunity to work on their list, we have more time to work on ours.

"Everything is Beautiful"

We have a perception or make a statement that something or someone is ugly. If we look at an insect up close, it may seem ugly. If we step back and look at the whole insect, we can see its beauty. Often as we observe it in action, the insect becomes even more beautiful. How are we looking at ourselves? Do we think we are ugly?

Actually, nothing is born ugly. Ugly is something we create by our attitude and behavior. Don't you remember your mother saying, "Don't be ugly!" She was referring to our behavior or words. Jesus said, " . . . What goes into someone's mouth does not defile them, but what comes out of their mouth, that is what defiles them." (Matt 15:11) He was saying that we can be harmful with our words and become ugly.

True beauty comes from within. "Beauty is not in the face; beauty is the light in the heart."[107]

We see things in nature that we say are ugly, like worms, spiders, or one animal killing another. The beauty or ugliness in such things is in our perspective. These acts and beings are part of a system created by a wise

---

106. *Alcoholics Anonymous*, 59.
107. Gibran, Lebanese Writer and Poet, 1883 to 1931.

creator. Genesis states in the first chapter, "God saw all that he made, and it was very good." (Gen. 1:31)

So the next time you see "ugly," step back and look at it from a different perspective. You may suddenly see the beauty in it or them. This is especially true when looking at oneself. Deep within, we are all beautiful. Sometimes we allow that seed of beauty to be covered over with the others' opinions, those who haven't taken time to look deep into our soul.

One of my favorite sayings came from Ethel Waters, the blues and jazz singer who once said, "God don't make no junk."

Time in the Desert

There are times when we feel God's absence. It feels like being all alone in a barren wasteland, a desert. The word *desert* comes "from the Late Latin *desertare,* frequentative Latin *deserere,* "to abandon, to leave, forsake, give up, leave in the lurch. . . . "[108]

When we feel that God is absent, nothing looks bright. We feel abandoned, hopeless, isolated, and disconnected from everyone. Often we think everything is for naught. No one likes being in such a desert. When we feel like we have hit rock bottom, where are we able to go? We may not think we have the motivation to go anywhere. So we just sit at the bottom, feeling like we are in a constant rut. An American Indian named Two Feathers said, " . . . a rut is just a grave with both ends knocked out.[109]

These images feel and sound hopeless. And yet, some miraculous transformations have taken place in the middle of such a desert, even when we have felt there was nowhere else to turn. Going through seemingly impossible experiences and emotional upheavals can cause us to look at life differently. Our perception shifts suddenly as life takes on a whole new meaning. Sometimes we have to be stripped of a sense of security and comfort to be free of assumptions about reality and conditioned beliefs (those instilled in us at some previous time). Ask those who have had near-death experiences, serious accidents, or heart attacks.

Much of the time we seem to thrive on life's big, sensational, and/or stimulating experiences. We spend time and energy reaching for big goals and rewards for all our hard work. How meaningless it all becomes when we find ourselves in the middle of the desert alone.

108. Etymology, "desert."
109. Hawk, "Seed Plante," 20.

Musings

Don't lose hope. Sometimes life uses the experience to help us make room for a new direction in our journey. And, we don't walk this journey alone, even if we feel we have been abandoned. We have been promised a comforter.

A wise young lady once said, "... struggles are exactly what we need in our life. If we were to go through our lives without any obstacles, we would be crippled. We would not be as strong as what we could have been. Give every opportunity a chance, leave no room for regrets."[110]

"It's the God's Truth"

How often have you heard the statements, "It's the God's Truth," or "I am not lying to you" or other similar statements that attempt to convince the listener that what we are saying is true? On the other hand, have you been tempted to bend the truth by saying "it's just a little white lie" or "what they don't know won't hurt them."

The choice between truth and a white lie came up as I went to the Motor Vehicle office to get a tag for an automobile. Even though the car was used and I bought it from a relative, the state government still wants 9.5% of the amount I paid for it. I struggled with having to pay that tax.

I tried to justify not paying the full tax amount by telling myself that I don't want to support our elected officials' political trips that are just a front for parties or personal jaunts. Other reasons cropped up but no matter how I tried to justify not paying the full tax amount, I had a gut feeling that I would feel bad about not being truthful.

Is it possible to be untruthful and not be hurt? I doubt it! My experience has been that not telling the truth begins to chip away at our soul, the pure and sacred part of us that makes us human. We also may have to work hard to keep the lie alive so as not to be caught. That takes energy, and again eats away our beauty.

But who will know? I will.

---

110. Centeno, *SearchQuotes*, 1992 to 2011.

Be Here Now

Look not to what might be, but to what is!
For this is all that is real, the "what is"
    Bring yourself back from mental wanderings
    And be here now, immersed in just being
Refrain from labeling, planning, and foreseeing
And touch, smell, see, feel, taste, and hear
    Do not expend energy attempting to push the river
    This just builds petitions to keep us from this experience of what is real
Lie back feeling immersed in the buoyant
And silkened cradle of life's basic gifts
    Drink in the experience of the journey
    The sky, the banks, the trees, and surprises of the moment
To leave oneself through envy of another's place
Is to walk away from knowing the true love of self
    We've built conditioned structures around us
    We justify and twist them as rules of etiquette to hide our true selves.
We cram the spaces with empty sacks
Blocking the beauty that lies beyond
    Fear is the culprit that drives our rigid ways
    That stands in the way of real hearing, seeing, and being
Loving and trusting ourselves gives us the gift of allowing enough space
In our togetherness to really be heart to heart
    Do not weep over what will not be
    Look to the joys to be created in the moment
The pace to these new experiences is much slower
Their beauty has been hidden in that finish line of empty celebration.
    You've entered a strange new land
    There are opportunities here that could not fit in that now dim land of Yore

—Edward L. Boye, 2012

Epilogue

Catfish, Cornbread, and "Crazy" People

I finish these musings with a true story about how far love and belonging can carry us when we let go of a common protective façade—thinking we are normal and others are crazy.

A colleague and I serving chaplain internships in a mental facility had the idea of taking eight patients with severe mental disorders fishing—a little like Jack Nicholson did in the movie, *One Flew Over the Cuckoo's Nest*. We escorted them (with permission) from the locked ward unit to a nearby pond once a week for ten weeks to catch catfish. This story is about the final gathering:

Five-thirty Tuesday afternoon, Cory, Susan, and I were running around the activity building kitchen in preparation for a catfish meal for the Unit I fishing group.

"Do you know how to make cornbread, Susan?" I asked.

"No, I don't," she responded.

"We will never get this meal ready in time!" I said.

Susan suggested, "Maybe some of the patients could help."

"Hey, that's what this is all about. We all caught the fish. So it *should* be a joint effort," I said with private reservations about whether they would be stable enough to work together.

I rushed down to Unit I, rooms that seemed like vaults in a tomb, and found the group gathered in anxious anticipation.

Someone asked, "Chaplain, is it ready for us?" I told them. "No, we are all going to prepare this meal together." They looked at me with surprise and reservations.

We gathered outside the unit by my car. "Have you ever heard of cramming a car with nine adult people? I asked.

Epilogue

Duncan said, "That's what we did in Florida when I was back home!"

I responded with a smile, "Well, that is exactly what we are going to do in my old Mercury." "OK, pile in, five in the back and four in the front. Jimmy, you sit up here on Arlie's lap. He will tell you a story as we drive to the building. "Lenny, you have to sit on John's lap."

"Naw, I'll just walk," he said, looking at his shoes.

"No, we want you to join us. Come on, Lenny."

"Well, if I have to sit in somebody's lap, I am not going."

"That's up to you," I said.

He started back up the walk to the unit, stopped, and then turned around running back, "Ok, I'll join."

Up on the hill we went, eight plus one "crazy" people crammed in the car like pretzels. This group had such deep wounds that they normally shied away from others. But they were laughing, enjoying the closeness, and the touching. I had the feeling that something was happening here that was beyond the human condition.

As we entered the building, I anticipated chaos in the kitchen with eight patients, two chaplain trainees, and the social worker trying to prepare food in that small room.

Once we settled down, everyone took a job with no arguments, no hassle, and no weird behavior. Susan learned how to make coleslaw with Agnes leading the way. Larry, who usually wanted to do things his way, helped Betty mix cornbread batter. Cory and John fixed the field peas. Arlie and I rolled the thawed fish in cornmeal. Bill, Kevin, and Duncan set the table.

I stepped back, watching the activity and thought, "What is happening here? These are people with severe mental illness from a locked ward in a state mental hospital. They are working together, laughing, joking, and having normal conversation. But they are sick! We are not attending to their problems, their hallucinations, and their delusions. Suddenly, the greatest delusion of all became clear, my own!"

There was a long table with three platters filled with golden brown catfish, two bowls of field peas, two plates of cornbread, a large bowl of slaw, and eleven glasses of iced tea. Everyone was standing. Someone finally looked at me and said, "Preacher, you goin' to ask the blessin?" Spontaneously, Cory took Susan's hand, Susan took mine, and everyone connected in a circle. In my state of awe, I felt the presence of our oneness and the One who said "For where two or three are gathered in my name, there am I

Epilogue

with them." (Matt 18:20) I blessed our group, each person and their journey toward healing, and gave thanks for the Holy Spirit so obviously uniting us, and for the food.

As we sat down, I noticed that there were four places set on each side and one setting on each end. That was only ten. Then I noticed the stout old man who had once told me how much he missed having a catfish meal making a place for himself at another table.

Someone said, "Wait a minute! Arlie, we cannot have the catfish chef sitting by himself! Everyone eagerly moved around and made him a place between Cory and Susan.

The "vittles" were passed around. I said, "Arlie, someone said you had already eaten in the cafeteria." He looked up with a mouth full of cornbread, and grinned from ear to ear. During this feast, there were periods of laughter, joking, and expressions of pleasure about the food. There was also quiet with only the sound of chewing. It was during those times that I was most aware of the hunger and thirst of these people.

Toward the end of the meal Larry asked, "Who is responsible for all of this? I mean whose idea was it to take the group fishing, and then have this meal?" I replied, "Cory and I decided together." Larry announced, "I feel like the group should show their appreciation with a good hand." There was a moment of enthusiastic clapping. Then he said, "I've never seen as many people from Unit I as happy and having a good time as we are now. Everyone is usually sitting around bored or talking to themselves." Cory and I looked at each other fully aware of the tears of joy within us.

"Larry, you may not know this," I said, "but that is the best gift you and the group could give Cory and I, and also to Susan for her support."

Another gift was being part of Sonny's journey with the fishing. He had never been fishing but wanted to go with the group. One afternoon I asked Arlie and Sonny to help me clean the fish. While I was squatting there with a headless bloody fish body, Sonny asked with a twisted face, "You mean people eat that?"

I asked, "You don't think you could eat one of these?"

With a look of disgust, he said, "No. Are you kidding me?" I wondered where his father had been all of Sonny's life, and relived memories of my Dad and I in the back yard as he showed me how to clean those repulsive creatures.

During the meal, Sonny looked around at me with a grin on his face and said, "You know. These are pretty good!"

Epilogue

After the feast, we sat around visibly filled and satisfied in so many ways. The feeling I felt in that room was comparable to Sunday afternoons at my grandmother's farm when we sat on the front porch, dozing and telling stories with friends and family.

This experienced awakened me to my own illusions about cure and fixing. I felt like I had a glimpse of what Christ meant when he talked about drinking from the well that satisfies your thirst (John 14:4), and eating the bread of life (John 6:35). Pretense, barriers, fear, and certainly anger disappeared that evening in the community building of a fenced place designed to keep "crazy" people where we think they need to be.

—Ed

Bibliography

Alcoholics Anonymous, 3rd Edition. Alcoholics Anonymous World Services, Inc. New York, NY: 1976.
Bailey, Elisabeth Tova. *The Sound of a Wild Snail Eating.* Thorndike, Maine: Center Point 1976 Large Print Edition, Algonquin Books, 2010.
Bible Gateway.com. Grand Rapids, Michigan: Zondervan. Online: http://www.biblegateway.com/
Bible Hub.com. Online: http://biblehub.com/greek/264.htm.
Bracket Jr., Joseph. "Simple Gifts" song, 1848.
BrainyQuote.com. "Darrow, Clarence." Accessed June 27, 2014. Online: http://www.brainyquote.com/quotes/quotes/c/clarenceda154026.html.
———. "Hubbard, Elbert." Accessed June 27, 2014. Online: http://www.brainyquote.com/quotes/authors/e/elbert_hubbard.html.
———. "Michelangelo." Accessed June 29, 2014. Online: http://www.brainyquote.com/quotes/authors/m/michelangelo.html.
———. "Moyers, Bill." Accessed June 3, 2014. Online: http://www.brainyquote.com/quotes/quotes/b/billmoyers382588.html.
Buechner, Frederick. *Whistling in the Dark: An ABC Theologized.* San Francisco: HarperCollins, 1988.
Cambridge Dictionary.org. Online. Accessed June 29, 2014. Online: http://dictionary.cambridge.org/us/dictionary/american-english/tenacious?q=tenacity.
Cook, David. *Seven Days in Utopia.* Arc Entertainment, 2011.
Diagnostic and Statistical Manual of the American Psychiatric Association, Fourth Edition. Washington, D.C., 1994.
Dictionary.com. "Truth." Accessed June 29, 2014. Online: http://dictionary.reference.com/browse/truth?s=t.
———. "Reality." Accessed January 29, 2014. Online: http://dictionary.reference.com/browse/reality?s=t
Education-Portal.com. "The Silent Generation: Definition, Characteristics, and Facts." Accessed June 29, 2014. Online: http://education-portal.com/academy/lesson/the-silent-generation-definition-characteristics-facts.html#lesson.
Encarta World Dictionary. Accessed February 15, 2014. Online: http://encarta-world-english-dictionary.software.informer.com/.
Facebook.com. "Peters, John A." Accessed April 6, 2014. Online: https://www.facebook.com/TheGreatSpirit.God/posts/570291626396602.

Bibliography

Geoff Fox. *My Permanent Record.* Accessed January 7, 2014. Online: http://www.geofffox.com/MT/archives/2011/12/17/sad-news-about-mike-wallace.php.

Gerrold, David. *Zen and The Art of Whatever.* Accessed June 29, 2014. Online: http://www.taoism.net/articles/zenart.htm.

Goodreads.com. "Allen, Woody." Accessed June 27, 2014. Online: http://www.goodreads.com/quotes/87478-if-you-want-to-make-god-laugh-tell-him-about.

———. "Dalai Lama XIV." Accessed June 27, 2014. Online: http://www.goodreads.com/quotes/103551-we-can-never-obtain-peace-in-the-outer-world-until.

———. "Gibran, Kahil." Accessed June 27, 2014. Online: http://www.goodreads.com/quotes/search?utf8=%E2%9C%93&q=beauty+is+not+in+the+face&commit=Search.

———. "Langbridge, Fredrick." Accessed June 27, 2014. Online: https://www.goodreads.com/author/quotes/3508961.Frederick_Langbridge.

———. Markham, Edwin. "Outwitted." Accessed June 27, 2014. Online: http://www.goodreads.com/quotes/8703-he-drew-a-circle-that-shut-me-out—heretic.

———. Markham, Edwin. "The Man with a Hoe." Accessed June 27, 2014. Online: http://www.goodreads.com/author/quotes/179023.Edwin_Markham.

———. "Osler, William physician, 1849 to 1919." Accessed June 27, 2014. Online: http://www.goodreads.com/quotes/412345-think-not-of-the-amount-to-be-accomplished-the-difficulties.

———. "Rogers, Will." Accessed June 27, 2014. Online: http://www.goodreads.com/quotes/42553-too-many-people-spend-money-they-haven-t-earned-to-buy.

Google.com search. Online: https://www.google.com/.

Grimm, Jacob, and Wilheim Grimm. *Grimms Household Tales.* Translated by Margaret Hunt. Online: http://www.cs.cmu.edu/~spok/grimmtmp/.

Harris, Alex H. S., and Thoresen, Carl E. Online: http://hpq.sagepub.com/content/10/6/739.short. *Journal of Health Psychology*, Dec. 2005 10: 739-752.

Hawk, Kevin Laughing. *Two Feathers, Spiritual Seed Planter.* Twin Lakes, Wisconsin: Seven Coin, 2003.

Kramer, Stanley. "It's a Mad, Mad, Mad, Mad World" movie. Hollywood, Los Angeles, California: Revue Studios, 1963.

Lathem, Edward Connery, Editor. *The Poetry of Robert Frost.* New York: Holt, Rinehart, and Winston, 1969.

Lawrence, Jerome. American Playwright and author, 1915 to 2004.

Lipton, Bruce, PhD. "Biology of Belief: Unleashing the Power of Consciousness, Matter, and Miracles." Fullerton, California: Elite, Mountain of Love, 2005. Accessed June 29, 2014. Online: http://www.thetruthaboutfoodandhealth.com/healtharticles/biology-of-belief-bruce-lipton-genes-cell.html.

Lorenz, Edward N. ScD. "Predictability: Does the Flap of a Butterfly's Wings in Brazil Set Off a Tornado in Texas?" Cambridge, Massachusetts, 1972. Accessed June 29, 2014. Online: http://eaps4.mit.edu/research/Lorenz/Butterfly_1972.pdf.

Macleish, Archibald. Accessed June 29, 2014. Online: http://www.enginesofmischief.com/makers/evan/sigs/politics.html.

Marche, Stephen. "Is Facebook making us lonely?" *The Atlantic Magazine*, 309:(4), 2012.

Martin, Nancy Lynn. "Life's Door." Bloomington, Indiana: iUniverse, 2009. Accessed June 29, 2014. Online: http://books.google.com/books?id=nre2tysx_FYC&pg=PR3&dq=nancy+lynn+martin&hl=en&sa=X&ei=W5QxU4rUDcLN2AWnjYDgCQ&ved=0CDUQ6AEwAg#v=onepage&q=nancy%20lynn%20martin&f=false.

Bibliography

MayoClinic.org. Accessed June 29, 2014. Online: http://www.mayoclinic.org/healthy-living/stress-management/in-depth/stress-relief/art-20044456

Merriam-Webster Dictionary, an Encyclopedia Britannica Company. Online: http://www.merriam-webster.com.

———."Pack." Accessed June 27, 2014. Online: http://www.merriam-webster.com/dictionary/pack.

———. "Content." Accessed June 27, 2014. Oneline: http://www.merriam-webster.com/dictionary/content.

———. "Temptation." Accessed June 29, 2014. Online: http://www.merriam-webster.com/dictionary/temptation.

———. "Tenacity." Accessed June 29, 2014. Online: http://dictionary.cambridge.org/us/dictionary/american-english/tenacious?q=tenacity.

———. "Twitter." Accessed June 29, 2014. Online: http://www.merriam-webster.com/dictionary/twitter.

Microsoft Word 2010. Encarta Microsoft Multimedia Encyclopedia, multimedia digital encyclopedia produced by Microsoft Corporation (1993–2009). CD-ROM.

———. "joy." Accessed January 23, 2014.

Niebuhr, Reinhold. *The Essential Reinhold Niebuhr: Selected Essays and Addresses*, edited by Robert McAfee Brown. Connecticut: Yale University Press, 1987.

Online Etymology Dictionary. "desert." Accessed June 29, 2012. Online: http://www.etymonline.com/index.php?allowed_in_frame=0&search=desert&searchmode=none.

Ornish, Dean. "Heart disease study." Accessed June 29, 2014. Online: http://www.pmri.org/dean_ornish.html.

Oxford Dictionaries.com Accessed June 27, 2014. Online: http://www.oxforddictionaries.com/us/definition/american_english/mindful.

Pascal, Blaise. *Pensées* #233. Translated by W.F. Trotter. Accessed June 27, 2014. Online: http://oregonstate.edu/instruct/phl302/texts/pascal/pensees-contents.html.

Peck, M. Scott, MD. *The Road Less Traveled*. New York: Touchstone, Simon and Schuster, 1978.

QuoteGarden.com. "Author unknown."Accessed January 28, 2014. Online: http://www.quotegarden.com/smiles.html.

Rilke, Rainer Maria. *Letters to a Young Poet*. New World Library, Novato, California, 2000.

Robinson, Phil Alden. *Field of Dreams*. Boston, Massachusetts: Gordon Company, 1989.

Sanskrit Documents. "Namaste." Accessed June 29, 2014. Online: sanskritdocuments.org/articles/Hindu_Rituals.pdf.

SearchQuotes.com "James Baldwin." Accessed March 10, 2014. Online: http://www.searchquotes.com/search/james+baldwin/.

———. "Casey, Karen, Author." Accessed April 3, 2014. Online: http://www.searchquotes.com/quotation/Truly_loving_another_means_letting_go_of_all_expectations._It_means_full_acceptance,_even_celebratio/28332/.

———."Centeno, Junethea Crystal." Accessed February 3, 2014. Online: http://www.searchquotes.com/.

Servo, Tom. "Infants Die If They Are Not Touched." Yahoo Contributor Network

Shakespeare, William. "All's Well That Ends Well" play (Act II, Scene I, 145-147). Online: http://thinkexist.com/quotation/oft_expectation_fails-and_most_oft_where_most_it/177378.html.

Shakespeare, William. "Hamlet." Act 3, Scene 2, 222-230. Online: http://www.enotes.com/shakespeare-quotes/lady-doth-protest-too-much-methinks.

Bibliography

Shakespeare, William, "Hamlet." Act 1, Scene 3, Page 3. Accessed January 24, 2014. Online: http://nfs.sparknotes.com/hamlet/page_44.html.

Taylor, Daniel. *Myth of Certainty: The Reflective Christian and The Risk of Commitment.* IVP Books, 1999.

The Free Dictionary by Farlex. Accessed June 27, 2014. Online: http://www.thefreedictionary.com/atavism. *The New Lexicon Webster's Dictionary of the English Language.* New York, 1987.

Thesaurus.com. "Coincidence." Accessed June 29, 2014. Online: http://thesaurus.com/browse/coincidence.

Thoreau, Walden. Accessed June 14, 2014. Online: http://thoreau.library.ucsb.edu/thoreau_walden.html.

Twentieth Century Fox, *The Best Exotic Marigold Hotel.* Blueprint Pictures, May 2012.

UrbanDictionary.com. Accessed June 29, 2014. Online: http://www.urbandictionary.com/define.php?term=Germaphobe.

Ward, William A. "Risk." Accessed March 14, 2014. Online: http://quotationsbook.com/quote/47971/.

Widener, Chris, "The Angel Inside Michelangelo, Il Gigante, and Creating a Life of Power and Beauty." Chris Widener: 2004. Accessed April 24, 2014. Online: http://www.asamanthinketh.net/files/The%20Angel%20Inside%20Ebook.pdf.

Wikipedia, The Free Encyclopedia. "Anonymous proverb." Accessed January 10, 2014. Online: http://en.wikiquote.org/wiki/Dr._Seuss.

———. "Aura." Accessed June 29, 2014. Online: http://en.wikipedia.org/wiki/Aura_(paranormal).

———. "Baby Boomers." Accessed April 23, 2014. Online: http://en.wikipedia.org/wiki/Baby_boomers.

———. Burns, Robert. "To A Louse, On Seeing One On A Ladies Bonnet At Church." Accessed January 14, 2014. Online: http://en.wikipedia.org/wiki/To_a_Louse.

———. "Fawcett, John, DD, British theologian, 1772." Accessed January 5, 2014. Online: http://en.wikipedia.org/wiki/John_Fawcett_(theologian).

———. Livingston, Jay and Evans, Ray. "Que, Sera, Sera." Accessed January 10, 2014. Online: http://en.wikipedia.org/wiki/Que_Sera,_Sera_(Whatever_Will_Be,_Will_Be).

———. "Mote, Edward." Accessed March 7, 2014. Online: http://en.wikipedia.org/wiki/Edward_Mote.

———. "American Indian Elder." Accessed June 27, 2014. Online: http://en.wikipedia.org/wiki/American_Indian_elder.

———. "This too shall pass." Accessed June 27, 2014. http://en.wikipedia.org/wiki/This_too_shall_pass.

———. Woolston, C. Herbert. "A Christian Child's Prayer." Accessed March 7, 2014 Online: http://en.wikipedia.org/wiki/Christian_child's_prayer.

———. Yogi, Maharishi Mahish. "Transcendental Meditation." Accessed April 6, 2014. Online: http://en.wikipedia.org/wiki/Transcendental_Meditation.

Williams, Margery, *The Velveteen Rabbit.* Accessed June 29, 2014. Online: http://digital.library.upenn.edu/women/williams/rabbit/rabbit.html.

Woodbury, Sarah. *Daughter of Time: A Time Travel Romance.* The Morgan-Standwood, Amazon Digital Services, Inc., 2011.

Yancy, Philip. *The Jesus I Never Knew.* Nashville, Tennessee: Harper Collins, 2008.

YourDictionary.com. "enchantment." Accessed June 29, 2014. Online: http://www.yourdictionary.com/enchantment.

www.ingramcontent.com/pod-product-compliance
Lightning Source LLC
Chambersburg PA
CBHW062027220426
43662CB00010B/1513